T0354362

Forever Laced

A Journey through Two Centuries

Kathryn Smith Lockhard

iUniverse, Inc.
New York   Bloomington

Forever Laced
A Journey through Two Centuries

iUniverse books may be ordered through booksellers or by contacting:

iUniverse
1663 Liberty Drive
Bloomington, IN 47403
www.iuniverse.com
1-800-Authors (1-800-288-4677)

Because of the dynamic nature of the Internet, any Web addresses or links contained in this book may have changed since publication and may no longer be valid. The views expressed in this work are solely those of the author and do not necessarily reflect the views of the publisher, and the publisher hereby disclaims any responsibility for them.

ISBN: 978-1-4502-3375-0 (sc)
ISBN: 978-1-4502-3377-4 (dj)
ISBN: 978-1-4502-3376-7 (ebook)

Library of Congress Control Number: 2010907685

Printed in the United States of America

iUniverse rev. date: 6/11/2010

Front cover photo: Mathias Roesch Homestead, Potosi, Wisconsin

Table of Contents

ACKNOWLEDGEMENTS

I'm forever grateful to my mother, Elsie Louise Roesch Smith, for sharing her memories with me, and my dad, Robert Franklin Smith, for teaching me the importance of family.

To all the many wonderful cousins and others I have met during my research, thank you. We have shared stories and photographs that allowed us to expand our family history together: Clyde Roesch, Russell Roesch, Paul Roesch, Ora Lee (Seawright) Palmer and Isabel Hart Williams, all of Florida, and to Janice Roesch, John Roesch, Lois Macke, Leslie Cardey Louthain and Kimberly Moore, all of Wisconsin and Kathleen Wolfe of the Potosi Township Historical Society and board member of the Passage Thru Time Museum in Potosi. Also, thank you to Patricia Braddock Youngs of Idaho, and Celine Mercier of France.

Other information was gathered from the following: the diary of Philip Roesch, family letters, newspapers, books, memoirs and organizations, the *Eau Gallie Record*, Eau Gallie, Florida; *Melbourne Times*, Melbourne, Florida; *Cocoa Tribune*, Cocoa, Florida; *Star Advocate*, Titusville, Florida; The *Oshkosh Northwestern*, Oshkosh, Wisconsin; *Grant County Herald*, Lancaster, Wisconsin and from articles written by Weona Cleveland, retired journalist of the *Florida Today*; *The Pulse*, of Saint Paul's United Methodist Church of Eau Gallie, Florida; the Brevard Historical Society, Cocoa, Florida and last but not least Ancestry.com.

DEDICATION

To my husband Merrill, thank you for sharing and experiencing this joyous adventure of genealogy. We have learned much about each other. A special thank you to my daughters, Tracey, Kimberly and Tiffany, and son, Merrill Jr., I appreciate your enduring patience. I love you all dearly.

IN LOVING MEMORY

My father, Robert Franklin Smith, passed away on the first day of spring, March 20, 2008 in Massachusetts, and my uncle, Russell Sterling Roesch, passed away in Florida on April 28, 2009. They will remain always in my heart.

EPIGRAPH

"We become who we are because of those that came before and the choices made. It is the results of those decisions that lace one generation to the next."

DISCLAIMER

The individuals in this book have been presented as accurately as possible through testimonies of those remaining. Certain story telling liberties have been taken, but events and facts surrounding the history are the result of actual, tireless research.

Introduction

_____

Footprints were left behind everywhere, in the sand, on the rocks, near the clear blue water's edge. If I blink, I fear I might miss seeing a fleeting memory rushing by at lightning bolt speed. Look closely under the surface, much like an archeologist mining for traces of history, a fragment of bone. Who are these spirits that taunt me? I keep digging deeper and faster yet to find my way home.

Gone from Eau Gallie, Florida is the city hall that once also housed the fire station and Police Department, the site marked only by a small blue plaque indicating where the local seat of government once stood; the unpretentious Post Office is no more, merged into the neighboring city of Melbourne. Yet even though those symbols of a formal close-knit community have vanished, residents to this day cherish this village, once the jewel of South Brevard County.

Eau Gallie sits neatly nestled along the oak and palm tree lined banks of the Indian River that merges with the Atlantic Ocean. The waning evening sun descends behind me casting ever-lengthening shadows upon the darkening water. I stand on the banks of the river, inhale deeply and the smell of salt and fish permeate my nostrils. I close my eyes and feel the wind tousle my hair as it wraps its arms around me and I am left with all my senses to wonder.

Gone are the early pioneers that arrived in the wilderness with slaves in tow. Gone too is the village's first mayor, the union soldier and the confederate sympathizer's daughter. Gone are the politicians, farmers, teachers and entrepreneurs who served their country and community well.

Who were these people that made willing sacrifices through the centuries as they fought wars, built communities, endured the loss of loved ones, suffered wounded hearts and broken marriages? Shrouded in mystery, trails

1

are left to disclose who they were, where they came from, and the purpose of their being.

The remnants left behind are the time-traveler tourists, searching for their place in history. Time doesn't stand still and tomorrow won't wait. A sigh, a blink, a wish upon a star and a century is gone.

This true story, rich in history, spans six generations of a family forever laced in love and life. They shared with us not only their personal, but also their public lives of military, political and community service. When this journey began, I could never have imagined all the many historical connections that would be revealed.

Finding one's ancestry is a journey of love and fascination. I say is, not was, because the search never ends, as one is always looking for another link, pursuing another story. Each ancestor or event uncovered feels as if one has found a piece of gold; excitement heightens and you never want the journey to end.

The Internet puts the world of information at your fingertips. Only occasionally do you find the need to travel much further than your own computer to locate documents across the United States or even out of the country. I have met cousins from Idaho, Wisconsin, Maine, Florida, France and places in-between. How exciting and wonderful to share photographs and stories of those who have gone before to help keep family histories alive.

To my amazement, my family ties are strongly embedded not only in Massachusetts, the state in which I live, but also in Florida, my birthplace. My roots are very well planted indeed and they travel far. I have traipsed through many cemeteries, from Canada to Florida, in the rain, having ruined many a pair of shoes.

As I uncovered my forefathers, their struggles, their sorrows, their successes and their failures, I discovered myself. Unveiling stories of the long hidden past has brought joy and a better understanding of who I am and brought ultimate peace. I felt as if I knew them personally and learned to value each of them for they are a part of me. Perhaps that has much to do with who I have become.

I had this strange sensation that they wanted to be found and was compelled by a strong force to forge ahead. *"Find me,"* I could hear their call. An obsession maybe; but only by uncovering my ancestral history could I begin to know who I truly am.

Sweet Aroma of Home

Franz Josef Rösch was born on March 21, 1771. He fought shoulder to shoulder with his brother in Napoleon's French Army for the Russian Campaign against the Fourth Coalition in the bloody Battle of Eylau (February 7–8, 1807). This battle left between 15,000 and 25,000 men wounded or killed. Franz was one of the many wounded on that savage winter's night near Moscow. His brother fortunately escaped injury. Everywhere you looked the snow was red with blood as soldiers lay dead, discharged like rag dolls.

That night, Franz and his brother, completely exhausted and weak from 14 straight grueling hours of battle, curled up together under a blanket to try and chase away the chill not only from their bones but from their minds as well. We imagine that as weary as they were, sleep would not come for the nauseating sounds and sights each experienced kept replaying the nightmare in their heads. To push away the horror of their thoughts, they spoke of longing for the sweet aromas of home as the frigid night wind howled, swirling snow around them. Finally they succumbed and welcomed sleep engulfed them.

The snow had ceased and the early morning sunlight came all too quickly, which woke Franz to the horror and ultimate despair upon discovering that his brother had frozen to death beside him.

Franz went home, and began collecting a pension for the gunshot wound he sustained to his arm. He married Maria Agatha Graf and they had six children. One can only imagine how the tragic events of his military encounter impacted Franz and how he imparted the wisdom and knowledge he gained to his sons, not to be fearful of defending justice in order to procure a better life for all. It became clear through generations that would follow that he emphasized the importance of family and told of the great sacrifice his brother had made, and he encouraged his children to live their lives in a way that would honor him.

His youngest child, Mathias Eugene Rösch, was born February 17, 1812 in Baden, Germany. Two years later, on January 2, 1814, when Mathias was only two years old, his father died at the age of 43. But Franz's story did not die with him. Surely Mathias' mother kept their father's memory alive by teaching all her children the values of life their father wanted them to embrace. Mathias would not forget.

Struggles of Daily Life

Mathias grew to be a strong yet gentle and soft-spoken man, a Rösch trait, and most likely stood slightly over six feet tall. According to written documents, his hair and full beard were both dark blonde and he had blue eyes. He married Magdalena Jehle, daughter of Ingaz Jehle and Regina Lorenz. Lena, as she was called, was born on June 13, 1814 in Baden, Germany and was one of 12 children.

Mathias and Lena bore 10 children: Joseph, Franz, Elenora, Philip, Regina, Herman, Felix, Magdalena, Josephine and Maria Anna. They did their utmost to care for their children who they dearly loved. Lena, like her mother, was a talented seamstress. Her nimble fingers were quick with a needle and thread, swiftly piecing together clothing for their growing children. Daily chores of cooking, cleaning and sewing kept her busy with little time for herself.

Mathias and Magdalena lived in the western foothills of the Black Forest on the banks of the Oos River and were fairly well off in a financial way. Mathias' home sat upon three acres of land.

Historical accounts of this era

Regina Lorenz and Ingaz Jehle with unknown grandchild,
Parents of Magdalena, Rosina and Christina
(Circa 1850)

report that well-to-do families lived in a large exposed half-timbered farmhouse with a thatched roof. They would also have had a barn to house their animals. The charming homes would be filled with simple yet delicate furniture and oil lamps provided light. The floors would have been of stone and walls of sandstone would be stenciled. Curtains would hang in the windows. The kitchen would be tastefully decorated with shelves to display their beautiful plates and other collectible items that adorned their home. Farmers of lesser means had dirt floors and shared their home with farm animals.

Mathias knew little when it came to farming, so this chore he delegated to his sons, according to memoirs written by his son Philip. Mathias was a "sacklermeiter", a master craftsman of leather clothing. He, with the help of his wife to keep up with the demand, made many a cap and mitten to keep their appreciative customers warm during the frigid winter months. The money he made was to purchase the hides of deer and other animals for his leather business, feed for the livestock and seed for the garden. He had all the work he could handle. Mathias hired Magdalena's cousin, Julianna Hodapp, to help his hardworking wife with the children and household chores. Julia, as she was called, in later years would play an even more important role in the lives of Mathias and his children.

The skill of plowing and planting the fields would not only see the family through some lean times in the years to come, but the children also gained insight as to the value of owning land. An acre of potatoes, a main staple, was planted and as it grew the fields would have been covered in white and pink blossoms turning the field into a flower garden. It produced enough potatoes to feed the family for a year. During the winter months the potatoes were stored in pits outside the house and would remain good to eat for about 10 months before they would rot. They also grew sun golden wheat that rolled like ocean waves in the breeze. There was a field of oats and a large vegetable garden to tend as well. Home life was good.

Due to a combination of fast population growth and harvest failure in 1846 and 1847, famine hit the area. During this devastating time, the fields would be watched diligently to make sure wild hogs and their own farm animals weren't able to get across the ravines dug around the crops. It was pitifully necessary to make sure peasants were not harvesting their fields for food. There were times when Mathias, the gentle man that he was, would share his bounty with a neighbor so much in need.

The boys shared the responsibility of chopping wood, not only for cooking but also for heating their home during the long cold winter months. Magdalena would have cooked on an open hearth that had no chimney. The smoke would rise preserving the bacon and sausages that hung from the low ceiling, until eventually the smoke found its way out of the house. A long rectangular table, most likely made from a fallen tree, would be sitting to the side of the hearth where this faithful family would have gathered together each day to give thanks for their bounty before each and every meal.

Magdalena's sister Rosina, also a talented seamstress and dressmaker, married Georg Ross. He was a saddler-shoemaker and dressmaker. Together, he and his wife worked at a renowned lunatic asylum, Illenau.

This asylum, located in Achern, Germany, opened in 1842 and was known to have great success with the healing of many. It was reputed that the success was due to the exemplary manner in which patients were treated and could have been in the forefront of today's treatments.

Rosina Jehle and husband Georg Ross with three of their sons.
Left to right: Eduard Georg b 1847, Otto Friedrch b 1849 August b 1852

Patients reportedly would take casual strolls around the colorful gardens growing on the property, enjoying the multitude of aromas and bountiful beauty. Doctors discovered early on that allowing patients to be involved in the planting, weeding and caring of the extensive grounds served a medicinal purpose. It seemed to calm the jittery, nervous patient and replaced frowns with smiles and a feeling of well being among others.

Often, groups would take excursions to various recreation areas. Trips were made to Mummelsee, a 55-foot deep lake considered to be of holy water.

It laid serenely snuggled at the foot of Hornisgrinde, the highest mountain at 3,820 feet, in the northern Black Forest of Germany. It was believed the lake was inhabited by Nix, a mythical spirit that had the ability to perform a metamorphosis of sorts by altering the body and mind, taking it to a better place.

Life was very hard for Rosina and Georg. It was one filed with strict customs within the institution. It was demanded that the rules of exhibiting sacrifice, service, eagerness and conscientiousness must prevail. Punishment would immediately follow any lack of discipline by any personnel. The focus of the institution was entirely on the care of their patients. Despite all this, Rosina and Georg were glad to submit to the regulations because of the enticement of great pay and the provision of a dwelling that sat on the institution's property. (Source: Economy-point.org)

With Heavy Heart

Church was the center of Mathias' family's social life. They were Methodists and they attended church faithfully. A proper upbringing and religious teachings of their children was important. The children were enrolled in Sunday school, and they received certificates of attendance that included their status in the class. These expressed the students' great diligence during religious lessons and good behavior.

Sadly, in 1850, death claimed their infant son Felix at the age of three months. The cause of death is unknown.

Mathias, according to written testimony by his son Philip, was a member of what was known as the Republican Party, working underground to overthrow the monarchy and to establish a republic in Germany. Mathias was willing to make whatever sacrifices necessary to advance the cause of unity, justice and freedom.

When the 1848 March Revolution began, Germany consisted of 39 states forming a Confederation. Its citizens were demanding freedom of the press and assembly and Baden was a center of revolutionary activities. A bill of rights had courageously been achieved, but all was reversed and lost by the time 1851 had come due to poor leadership, lack of funds and a preference of passive intellectual debate rather than violence.

Using facts from history as a guide, and actual accounts from memoirs, we can recreate a possible, if not probable, conversation between Mathias and his wife and of the emotions of the time.

"Lena," Mathias called late one night after the children were asleep, patting the mattress beside him, "come sit with me, we need to talk."

Lena walked over to her husband and sat beside him on their bed adjacent to the kitchen and looked searchingly into his soft blue eyes. "What is it

Mathias?" She could hear the concern in the tone of his voice. "Is something wrong, are you in trouble?"

"Everything is fine," Mathias continued. "We, in the underground, work diligently to resolve things peacefully. We all agreed, no violence. We will not behave in the manner of the monarchy. I am so weary of having no rights in this country. It's difficult to raise money for our cause. At times we're all fearful of who to trust. If I am not careful and I'm caught, at best I would be sentenced to prison for a very long time, or worse yet, executed.

"Our son Joseph is fast approaching military age. The German government will soon force him to become a soldier for their unjust cause." Mathias emphatically said, "I did not raise my boys to be soldiers in Germany." (Source: Philip Roesch)

"We have spoken many times about this and we need to prepare ourselves no matter how difficult we know it will be. I will speak to Joseph tomorrow night," said Mathias. "But right now, the Republican Party is waiting for me and night is the best time to leave so I can hide in the shadows and not be so easily seen. Don't wait up for me, I'll be late getting home."

Mathias walked out the door and Magdalena began to weep quietly, for she surely knew what her husband was implying. She began to slowly drift off to sleep as she recalled the many evenings they had spoken about the dream of a better life for their children. They had taught their sons to respect mankind, to fight against evil and for the things that were good and right. They spoke often of America and what they believed was a world of great freedom and opportunity. The German monarchy was one of oppression and wrong to keep its people hostage and afraid. Yes, she thought, some day that dream will come true.

The next morning Magdalena awoke early as usual to begin her first chore of the day by preparing a hearty breakfast before the daily tasks of working the farm began. Her heart stood still as she realized that Mathias was not beside her. She quickened her steps to find her husband sitting in his favorite chair staring out the window, watching the rising sun. He had arrived home later than usual and rather than disturb his wife he had fallen asleep fully dressed.

"What is it Mathias?" asked Lena of her husband as she knelt beside him, gently touching his hand.

Mathias replied, "I see no end in sight of a peaceful resolution and tonight I must say goodbye to my son." Lena gazed solemnly down toward the floor shaking her head ever so slightly to indicate she understood. She slowly rose and went to begin her daily chores.

The children were fed and the younger ones sent off to school. The older boys, Joseph and Franz, were sent to the garden to harvest the vegetables ready for picking. The few livestock necessary for family life had to be fed and the cows needed milking. The eggs were collected and a hen was to be slaughtered for Magdalena to clean and dress for dinner.

When these chores were done Joseph and Franz joined their father in his leather shop. The boys had become capable farmers and now their father was teaching them the business of being leather craftsmen as well. Along with learning the skills necessary to survive and earn a living, Mathias taught them through storytelling, just as his mother had with him, the importance of being good citizens, helping their neighbors, being honest men and working for what is fair and just. The boys were good students and made their father proud.

It had taken from sunup to sundown for all work to be completed in the house of Mathias. This day as usual Magdalena had given the girls lessons of sewing, running a kitchen and how to prepare and put a hardy meal on the table. The chicken dinner was prepared with much love and attention to detail for Lena knew what the night would bring.

All too soon the younger children were put to bed and Mathias beckoned Joseph to come. His son dutifully went to his father's side, hearing in his voice a sense of urgency.

Mathias began, "Joseph, many times we have shared the dream of freedom. I have prepared carefully for many years for my children to have a better life than your grandfather or me. You are fast approaching the age when you will be required to join the military. I am sending you to America and pray that you will remain safe. God will watch over you during your travel. Remember, if you need help you can always seek out your Aunt Christina.

"Once you get to America, write and let us know where you are. You can create a life with the skills I have taught you. You have prepared yourself well."

Joseph listened to his father intently, with a heavy pounding heart, for he did not want to leave; but he knew his fate was sealed in the truth his father spoke.

God Speed

Over the next two months in 1853, Mathias and Magdalena made preparations by obtaining a passport for their sixteen-year-old son so he might sail across the ocean to a new world and far away from them. Mathias was determined to do right by his children.

Magdalena would have packed his clothes and prepared food for her first-born son's long journey. It was the last act of love she could give him.

Joseph put forth a forced smile as he said goodbye to his siblings, telling them it would not be long before they were all together again. He would write. It must have been difficult to smile when he bade his weeping mother goodbye. Joseph would have turned quickly and walked out the door of the only home he had ever known for the last time, with tears in his eyes.

Waiting outside was his father. The horses were hitched to the wagon carrying all the necessary supplies needed for the journey ahead. Joseph climbed in and sat beside his father, and then slowly and quietly they rode away.

They arrived at the train station that would take Joseph to the port of Bremerhaven, in Bremen. Joseph and Mathias solemnly unloaded the wagon. They stood for just a moment facing each other, Joseph unsure of the future. Mathias firmly grabbed his son by the shoulders to reassure him that he could do this. "Goodbye, Joseph, have a safe trip and may God speed."

Joseph arrived in Manhattan, New York, presumably thinner after many weeks at sea. The journey was likely more difficult than he could have imagined and he undoubtedly was grateful to be on land once again.

Family records tell us that with the few pieces of gold his father had given him, Joseph would have boarded the train with others he had met on the ship and traveled with them and others to Wurtsboro. It was a small village north of Manhattan where many German families were settling because of its resemblance to the high mountain villages they left behind.

Here Joseph set his sights on beginning his new life. It was a place where he could live comfortably among others of German decent. He quickly obtained a job as a farm hand for the Devens family two miles north of Wurtsboro.

He wrote his father as promised to assure his family about his safe arrival and good fortune in finding work and friends. But the letters became less and less frequent until they were no longer, certainly much to the disappointment and worry of his parents.

A little over two years later, at the age of 19, Joseph began the trade of blacksmithing and eventually purchased the business where he worked.

The following year the situation continued to deteriorate in Germany. The rural economies were collapsing; jobs were being destroyed and countless farm laborers and artisans were thrown out of work.

History repeats and Mathias' second son, Franz, applied for his passport on December 19, 1854 to sail to America. He was described as age 17, blue eyes, with blonde hair, obvious traits he received from his father. But his chin, described as sharp, was indeed from his mother.

Franz's ship arrived in a place called New Orleans in early February 1855. He headed northwest until he reached St. Louis, Missouri. The area was primarily a frontier with vast tracts of heavily forested and unpopulated land. This locale was called Deutscheim, which means German home. Many German families were settling here, working diligently to reestablish that which had been most valued in their homeland.

But, Franz was not equipped to start anew in this place, it was winter and work was scarce. He heard about a city where there were more job opportunities. Franz would have taken the riverboat up the Mississippi and on to Chicago, Illinois before the money his father gave him was depleted. It wasn't long before he successfully found employment as an apprentice blacksmith. He vowed that someday he would return to St. Louis.

Over the succeeding years, Franz mailed many letters home to his parents from Chicago urging them to come. In one letter he told them "America is a nice, healthy country and land in Iowa sells at one and one-fourth dollars an acre."

Joseph, still living in New York, began writing home once again.

Three more years passed and nothing had changed in Germany. Work was always the same, the struggles the same, oppression the same.

Most likely Mathias was growing wearier by the day. One could easily believe that the strain was becoming unbearable.

Mathias, feeling defeated, gazed into space with sullen eyes, and said to Lena, "All these years and I feel like a failure. I have accomplished nothing."

Lena gently took hold of her husband's rounded chin in her slender fingers and turned his head ever so slightly to meet her comforting eyes. His eyes were as blue as ever, she thought; yet his dark blonde hair and always neatly trimmed beard now had streaks of gray and wrinkles were etched on his wide and worried brow.

"Mathias," she began, "you have always shown your love by providing for me and our children. You're a good husband, a good father and God has always lived in your heart. Our son Philip is now 14 years old and before long he too will be of military age. Mathias, please, let's all join Joseph and Franz in America. Franz writes that he wants us to come."

Mathias smiled, "You're right Lena, it's time to go."

Perseverance

Life would become very busy in the Rösch household over the next few months; the preparations seemed endless. The children would have been excited about the long journey ahead and sailing by ship across the ocean to join their brothers. The youngest of the children either didn't remember Joseph and Franz or they were born after they left for America. There was much curiosity among them about this new country they were going to and eager to help in any way they could. But, being so young, their little hands were most likely more of a hindrance than help.

The Mathias Roesch Family

| Philip | Charles | Otto | Magdalena (Roesch) Crouch | August | Sophia Luella (Roesch) Westing |
| John Albert | Mary Elizabeth (Roesch) Fine | Julia (Hodapp) | Regina (Roesch) Cardey | Joseph Eugene |

Roesch Children as Adults

Official records in Achern, Germany show that on March 29, 1857 Mathias and Magdalena applied for permission to sail to America with their remaining seven children. Eventually, they were able to make the required public announcement in the local newspaper of their intention to emigrate to America and their debts were cleared. Permission was finally granted and soon they would be on their way. (Announcements of the intention to emigrate Baden, Württemberg, and other states started around 1800.)

Their passport stated they wished "to take up residence in Northern America in order to establish permanent residence." It further stated, "domestic and civil military authorities are asked to let them pass."

Mathias sold his large home with three acres of land, his barn and animals. The money he received from the sale provided the funds necessary to begin again in America.

Mathias, at the age of 45, surely helped his wife pack up their trunks of clothing, utensils and quilts. They were required to bring their own staples to eat as they crossed the ocean. Food chests normally carried cured mutton, soft whey cheese and other salted or dried foods and flatbread. Kegs carried sour milk and beer.

Elenora

Elenora, their seventeen-year-old daughter, was now the eldest living at home. Apparently, Mathias and Magdalena had heard one too many rumors about young girls being preyed upon by sailors and they were concerned for her safety. They must do something, anything to protect her. Surely she is old enough to understand. The manifest gives us a hint as to what might have occurred.

Magdalena carefully cut her daughter's long dark blonde hair with all the love and understanding she could muster as she tried to ebb her daughters sorrow. She then handed Elenora a neatly folded shirt and a pair of pants that belonged to her brother. Her father presented her with a leather cap and vest he had made especially for her. Elenora, bravely holding back her tears, turned and silently carried the items to her room.

There surely was an air of anticipation mixed with some trepidation as the family boarded the William Nelson in LeHavre, France. Philip carried his six-month-old baby sister Maria, who was quite content to sleep away this big moment in her life, aboard in a clothesbasket. Elenora, appearing somewhat anxious that her masquerade would be exposed, boarded as Leopold, described as a male, age 17, and was recorded as such on the immigration records.

But, something else had changed too. Incorrectly recorded on the manifest was their surname. It went from Rösch, to Roesch. (pronounced Ray-shh)

The accommodations of tween decks, normally used for cargo, provided wide family bunks lined on either side of the ship, one above the other. There were many other families on this deck with trunks of their own, making little room to move about. Oil lamps were used to provide light in an otherwise dark environment, but *not* to be used during bad weather for fear of fire. Also, for safety, orders were issued as to when the oil lamps were to be shut off at night.

To prevent illness, the captain of the ship enforced strict rules regarding good hygiene. Many passengers, particularly during rough weather, suffered from seasickness and vomited on the vessel's wood plank floor. The stench alone caused others to fall ill.

On each end of the deck, you could always find a line waiting to use one of the two primitive oak barrel toilets that contributed to the odor that hung heavily in the air. Despite queasiness, passengers had to take on the responsibility of washing the floor with chlorine and vinegar to help deaden the worst smell.

In an attempt to foster good health, German ship captains required emigrants aboard to take exercise on deck. (Source, Jeff Hoffman.net)

On May 1, in the middle of the ocean, Philip turned 15 years old.

Their arduous journey lasted a very long and trying 46 days. They arrived slightly thinner and assuredly exhausted in New York on May 26, 1857. Upon reaching their destination, their fears began to dissipate and hope emerged once again. Spring had arrived and everything was in bloom. Their dreams were becoming a reality after so many years of political struggle. Finally, they had safely arrived in the land of freedom and opportunity, America.

Clyde Roesch, Mathias' grandson, wrote in a letter, "Finally, the German government gained a knowledge of the Republican Party and my grandfather got out of Germany just ahead of them."

About the William Nelson

The US ship "William Nelson" was built in Somerset, Massachusetts in the year 1850 and was financed by William Witlock Jr. of the City of New York. The William Nelson sailed its last voyage from the port of Antwerp on June 1st, 1865. On the 25th of June 1865 the ship caught fire, burned and sank with 426 German and Swiss immigrants aboard. The captain, Levi Smith, and his crew were the first to abandon the ship. Men woman and children were left to fend for themselves and die in fiery misery and confusion. Peter J. Schaps-Birgden of Germany was the eldest of seven children and traveling with his family, nineteen in all, and was the family's only known survivor. More information can perhaps be found about this ill-fated voyage recorded at the National Archives in the file of William H. Seward, Secretary of State. (Source: Immigrant Ships Transcribers Guild, Ship William Nelson, Harve, France to New York, January 2, 1857)

Westward Passage

Once docked in New York the family would have slowly disembarked, staying close together, making their way through crowds of other nervous but hopeful immigrants to begin their new lives. They surely stood patiently in endless long lines, finally clearing the processing center without incident at Castle Garden off the southwest tip of Manhattan.

Castle Garden Immigrant Landing Depot, the threshold to America, opened on August 3, 1855. During this early period, the only thing the federal government concerned itself with were questions regarding naturalization, sanitary conditions of the ship and the tabulation of foreign passengers entering their boarders.

Ship arrivals were published in the newspaper so friends and family knew when to come and meet the boat. It was common practice to have family members meet incoming relatives. It reassured the government that the immigrants had a place to go. Joseph, living in Wurtsboro, New York would have been the obvious to greet his parents and siblings when they arrived.

When Mathias and his family stepped outside, there was Joseph waiting in anticipation to welcome them. He then led them to the railroad ticket office. After a brief reunion, his parents, brothers and sisters boarded the train and Joseph waved as it pulled away.

Their trek would take them westward from New York City to Newark, New Jersey where they disembarked. Here they would rest and visit with Magdalena's sister, Christina, who had made her way to America in 1844, some 13 years earlier with her husband, Johannes Kreitler, now known as John. He ran a business with his brother, "Kreitler Brothers", a painting enterprise. It had to have been a joyous and tearful reunion, especially for the two sisters. So many years had gone by and so much to talk about in such a short time.

The 14 German-English schools in the area for their children to attend drew German immigrant families to Newark. The families may have had varying religious or political views, but all had strong convictions about preserving the German language for their children. It is singularly touching to note how the greater part of the less fortunate class were willing to make any sacrifice in order to grant their offspring an education in the German language. Over 3,700 children were receiving instruction in their mother tongue. (Source: Essex County, N.J. published with the cooperation of Citizens 1897, Early Settlement of Essex County, Chapter: Educational Institutions of Essex County)

It was time to catch the next train. The family continued it's journey northwest by railroad to Philadelphia, to Harrisburg, then on to Pittsburgh, Pennsylvania. From here the tracks led them to Mansfield, Ohio and through Sandusky, over to Toledo and into Chicago, Illinois, where they met up with their son Franz.

Franz told his father about Iowa and how it was great farming country and he should go there and grow wheat. However, Mr. Falert, a good friend, had informed Mathias of fertile soil for farming and excellent grazing land for livestock in Potosi, Wisconsin and persuaded him to go and buy a farm there.

Many families from the homeland have gone there, Mathias explained to his son. Furthermore, he was told that there was good drinking water and plenty of wood for cooking and keeping warm in the winter. *"There was no wood in Iowa,"* said Mathias. (Memoirs of Philip Roesch)

Many disappointed German patriots had gone to Wisconsin before them. They were called the Forty-Eighters due to the 1848 Revolution. They too had heard of fertile soil for farming and excellent grazing land for livestock.

Many German immigrants were fairly poor when they came to Potosi, Wisconsin. It was mainly a lead mining community at that time and the work paid the best wages. With little or no money, these displaced farmers had to mine sometimes up to 10 years before having enough money before returning to the land. It was their dream to buy a farm and be mortgage free.

It was in 1849 when gold was discovered in California. But, it wasn't until 1852 that the lead miners began a large exodus out of Potosi to head west, changing this commercial town into an agricultural community. (Source: The History of Potosi by Elda O. Baumann, The Wisconsin Magazine of History Vol. XXII Sept 1939)

Franz, now Americanized, was called Frank. He joined his family and together they traveled on to Galena, Illinois, located on the Wisconsin boarder. They crossed into Wisconsin and over to Potosi, arriving on June 6, 1857, exactly 12 days after arriving in New York.

Per Philip, "Father, Frank and Mr. Falert started out to hunt a farm and came over to Boice Creek. Mr. John Burton would sell his place where Sedbrook is now. Thomas O'Hara would sell his farm of 60 acres for $1,600. Sylvester Irish would sell 125 acres for $1,250, so father bought it. This amount was more than the average annual earnings a year of a factory worker."

It was agreed, as part of the deal, to the transfer of one cow and one calf, one sow, four stands of bees and five hens. Also included were a wagon and a yoke of oxen and some household goods. The farm had eight acres in cultivation and the rest was in timber. The agreement included all the crops—corn, wheat and potatoes—that were presently growing. The sale was dated and signed on June 11, 1857. (Source: Bill of Sale)

"Brother Frank stayed about a month, would not stay any longer," Philip wrote.

"By the following spring, father and I had cleared and plowed two acres and with the help of the oxen cleared away the stumps. We found the soil to be not much different than our farmland in Germany. We planted six acres of wheat in the old fields, but cinch bugs killed the crop. Our return was barely more than the money spent on seed."

"That fall there was a 'smash-up', all the banks went under and there was no money. Philip recalled, "Poor Mr. Irish had lent the gold he received from the sale of the farm to a storekeeper who went broke. All Mr. Irish got out of it was a horse.

"The house had an extremely leaky clapboard roof. When it snowed there was about as much snow up in the garret as there was outside. The other buildings on the property were built of logs.

"The following year it became necessary to do some repairs on the house. During that winter 16-inch blocks of wood were cut from black oak trees. The blocks were carried into the house in the morning to get the frost out by night. Then a wooden shaving horse was used to make shingles.

"We all had to live in a one-story building 12 by 20 feet until we got the house built up again…built up the large log hay and horse barn. All of those buildings only cost what nails we used on them, for I worked at the sawmill to pay for all the sawing. That was $5 a thousand. I and the oxen got $1.50 a day sawing logs. We always had plenty to eat, but money was very scarce."

Getting the farm up and running seemed endless and took a lot of muscle. There was no time to become politically involved and Mathias did miss it. But the fear and anxiety they lived with for so long in Germany was gone. No longer was there a need to lock the doors, no fear their animals or farm equipment would be stolen. Life was found to be quiet and safe in Potosi.

Every Beginning Has an Ending

Magdalena gave birth to one more child on January 14, 1860, a son, John Albert. Mathias must have been overjoyed at the thought of his newborn son being the first Roesch American citizen. Now truly America was home.

A year later, in late March of 1861, Magdalena became ill with a cold. Her cough deepened and sharp pains ripped though her chest. She was ordered to bed when the fever hit, but her health continued to deteriorate. Her breathing became labored and nothing seemed to ease her suffering. Now she was sleeping more than she was awake.

Mathias and the children surely gathered closely around her. The time was drawing near to say a final goodbye. Sadly, in the early spring, April 14, 1861, Magdalena, at the age of 46, took her last breath and died of pneumonia. Elenora carried the babies, one-year-old John Albert and Marie, age three, over to kiss their mother goodnight. The other children followed, kissing their stilled and quiet mother ever so gently with love for the very last time, leaving teardrops upon her cheek. The children all slipped quietly from the bedroom and their father slowly closed the door behind them. He pulled his chair quietly closer to the bed and took his wife's small hand, still warm to the touch in his, and kissed it ever so softly. He then laid his head upon her and wept. His precious Lena was gone.

Church services were held as family and neighbors mourned her death, with burial following in Dutch Hollow, Wisconsin, her final resting place, a few miles east of their Potosi home. Lena had gone home to her maker. (Around 1913 the town's name was changed from Dutch Hollow to Tennyson, after the English poet, Lord Alfred Tennyson.)

"Times had been hard since arriving in 1857," said Philip. 'I worked outside the home lots of days during that time. All a man could get was 50 cents a day and a day's work was from sunup to sundown. Wheat flour was selling for $5 a hundred so it would take 10 days to earn 100 pounds of flour. Good farm hands would earn $10 to $13 a month."

Elenora married Ignatius Stoll on November 26, 1861, seven months after her mother's death. Now that Elenora was married, fifteen-year-old Regina was expected to care for her baby brother, and younger sisters, plus manage the household and all the duties that it encompassed. She did the very best she knew how from all she had learned from her mother.

Mathias needed a wife and his children needed a mother. Mathias sent for Magdalena's cousin, Julianna. He knew her very well; she had worked at their home in Germany and the children were very fond of her. Julia, as she was called, was a gentle, sweet woman with black-brown hair and brown eyes. She was 16 years younger than Mathias and from his hometown. (Family memoirs)

On March 16, 1862 Julianna Hodapp, at the age of 34, purchased her ticket for 82 gulden with the money Mathias sent her. She boarded the ship Tigres, sailing third class. Her passport stated she was coming to earn a living in America. Julia arrived in New York on the 5th of May.

She was a plain, petite woman, wearing her hair pulled taut into a bun. She was donned in a high-collared black dress that covered her ankles and black shoes peaked out from beneath her skirt. Around her shoulders she wore a black wool cape that tied at the neck to keep her warm.

Julia spoke no English and was most likely quite nervous. But we suspect that Joseph was there to meet her as she disembarked the ship. He would have warmly greeted her and quickly she was made to feel comfortable. "Danke schön," said Julia, as she sighed with relief and smiled. He would have led Julia to the train, carrying her two oversized black duffel bags. He saw her safely off to Potosi where the family surely greeted her with genuine affection.

On May 11, 1862, six days after her arrival, she and Mathias were married, one year and one month from the anniversary date of Magdalena's death. All the children attended and celebrated the joyous union. Julia would give her husband five more children: four sons, Charles, Louis, Otto (pronounced Oh-toe) and August; and one daughter, Sophia. Mathias had now been blessed with a total of 15 living children.

Mathias' Homestead, Potosi, Wisconsin
August, Julia and Otto Roesch

Patriotism Lives On

Abraham Lincoln, opposed to slavery, was elected President in 1860. The southern states felt threatened and began to pull out of the union starting with South Carolina. This snowballed into six more states seceding with four more threatening to do so. The situation continued to deteriorate leading to the onset of the Civil War that began on April 12, 1861. Lincoln's call to arms went out, "In this great moment in the history of the United States there are no Irish, no Germans, no Scandinavians, no aliens, but only Americans."

Mathias' sons were very patriotic and never forgot the lessons of freedom they were taught. No, they were not meant to be soldiers in Germany, but the moment they heard there was trouble in America, four brothers enlisted and became Union soldiers for the preservation of the Union and freedom for the oppressed and the underprivileged.

Joseph Eugene Roesch served three years with honor, in Company I, 54th Regiment, New York Volunteers and at the close of the war he held a lieutenant's commission. He returned home to Wurtsboro, New York. On September 11, 1859 he married Rachel Ann Smith. He and Rachel had 10 children.

"He was a highly respected resident of this village. He was a member of the General Lyon Post, G. A. R. of Middletown. When Waterbury Post of Wurtsboro was in existence he was a very active member and for a time was its commander. He was school trustee for about 15 years; was village trustee at different times and its president in 1902 and 1903. He was a volunteer fireman and member of the Hook & Ladder Co. No. 1. He was first assistant chief of the fire department and for a time was acting chief.

"Politically involved, Joseph was a staunch Republican but never sought public office. He was a coroner for two consecutive terms and acted as such in the famous murder cases of Peddler Hutch in 1890 and Mrs. Halliday in 1903. In every official position that Joseph held, were filled with honor and benefit to the community and credit to himself."

"He was also found in any movement for the betterment of the village in which he lived. He was honest and industrious and was always one of the first and most generous to any benefit that he considered good.

"Joseph Eugene Roesch, at the age of 70, died of chronic gastritis at his home on Sunday, April 30, 1905. The funeral was held at 1 p.m. in his home on Kingston Avenue and interment followed in Sylvan Cemetery in Wurtsboro. His wife preceded him in death on October 2, 1903." (Excerpts from his Obituary)

Their son, Joseph, Jr., became a lawyer and later was appointed Chief Justice of the Supreme Court in Albany, New York.

———

At some point Frank left Chicago and moved to St. Louis, Missouri. It was here he enlisted in the Union Army and was stationed for three months at Siegel, Missouri, then joined the 4th Missouri Calvary and served three years. He was the only brother to be wounded.

It was on September 7, 1865 that Frank wrote a letter to his brother at the end of the Civil War, from Louisville, Kentucky.

"Dear Brother:

"The letter which Regina and you wrote to me July 31st I received already in Columbus Ohio. I would have written sooner but I did not know what I should write about. The military as it operates I cannot write to you but you know as much about it as I do.

"It caused me great joy that I noticed in your letter that you are all well. Regina also wrote to me that she met Louis, Phil and Herman at a ball.…. Such news also caused me joy because as long as a person is young he must learn to appreciate his younger years, because they do not last very long.

"I received about three months ago the cold fever while we were yet living in Columbus and still are not rid of it today. I have this fever not alone, but about half of the company had brought this over here. Columbus was a very unhealthy place. Morning from nine until eleven o'clock is generally the time when the bedstead shakes. I have it only every other day, but then I am so all in that I feel as if I had lost five pounds.

"A little while ago I wrote to St. Louis for medicine to a well-known doctor and yesterday I received it and I am convinced that in the next few days I will be rid of it because this noble doctor had prescribed this for my fever previously. Our regiment doctor gives everyone (the same medicine) out of the identical bag regardless of what is wrong. Under these circumstances we could have our bodies destroyed or have the fever or something else, that's the way it is all over.

"About mustering us out, there is no order yet. On top of this there is absolutely nothing that we have to do, but we still run around just as soldiers. Besides this, we are nearly no longer human beings. Philip, you have bought some. I also want to get onto the land and I want you to known this because I have made up my mind that I want to go onto the land.

"There are several in my company who have won for themselves a place in music because a Methodist preacher has been visiting this company. With his gift of gab he makes them believe anything and that he can obtain for them and naturally expects them to pay him for it.

"The whole company will soon be on furlough. Some are already gone. In twenty days I might come to you and live with you and then we could be our alone in conversation after which we can look over the land.

"I greet everyone and I expect an answer soon."
Frank Roesch

Once finally discharged, Frank joined the new army corps called Hancock's Corps, for two years and immediately received a $300 bounty. He was then assigned to the district in which he lived, St. Louis, Missouri. Frank, with his $300 coupled with other savings, purchased his land and went into farming just as he longed to do. He married Mathilda Wirth on July 16, 1878. Frank passed away in 1912.

———

On October 15, 1864, Herman enlisted in Company A, 12th Infantry Regiment Wisconsin, called the Marching Twelfth. He was in the March from Atlanta to the Sea and attended the Grand Review. He mustered out July 16, 1865 in Louisville, Kentucky. He moved to St. Louis, Missouri where his brother Frank was living. Herman, at the age of 50 married for the first time to Julia Anna Dorothea Frdiese on June 20, 1895. He practiced the Catholic religion, the faith of his wife. They had no children. He too enjoyed life as a farmer.

In 1910, when he was 65 years of age, he entered the United States National Home for Disabled Volunteer Soldiers suffering from asthma and bronchitis. The facility was initially for Civil War Veterans, but later accepted vets from the War of 1812 and then WWI. In 1930 the name was changed to the Veterans Administration Hospital to serve all Veterans.

Herman was described as five feet five inches tall, having gray eyes and gray hair, a farmer by trade. Nine years later, on August 23, 1919, he died of renal failure. Herman was collecting a pension of $32 a month at the time of his death. His personal effects totaled $590.25. He bequeathed this money to his youngest brother, John Albert Roesch, who was living in Potosi, Wisconsin with his wife Susan Taylor, son Lake and daughter Iona. Herman was buried in the Danville National Cemetery in Danville, Illinois.

———

August 6, 1862, Henry Coons, Justice of the Peace at Potosi, Wisconsin, swore Philip into service. Philip joined the Union Army's Co. H, 25th Regiment, Wisconsin Volunteers on the 11th of August 1862. He was at the siege of Vicksburg, the Atlanta Campaign under General Sherman and the March to the Sea. Philip attended the Grand Review in Washington, D.C. and paraded down Pennsylvania Avenue.

Philip kept a diary all during the nearly three years of his service, from August 6, 1862 to his discharge on June 11, 1865. This diary, handwritten in German, was translated and published in Midland, Michigan, by R. K. Long in 1979. The original and the translated version are in the Library of Congress. Selected excerpts of his diary follow:

"We camped at Richmond all night and arrived at Paynesville on the 5th. When we first went into camp they gave us one tent to every ten men. The boys played cards at night. One man, by the name of Andrew Jackson from Beetown, a stranger to us, was put in our tent. He did not like to see us playing cards, so he said he would teach us to read and write, and that stopped the card playing. This was the only English education I ever received.

"We camped at Richmond all night and arrived at Paynesville on the 5th. These places were small towns. There were the two companies, H and E of Platteville, at this place. The other three companies were sent to Sauk Center and other places.

"Here we found a fort the people had built of prairie sod. They plowed the sod, then cut it into lengths about two feet long, and built a wall like a stonemason would build, leaving portholes to shoot through. Grain, that had been ripe for months, was standing up nice and the farmers came and cut and threshed it. There had been three houses in the fort but there was only one left because the Indians had surprised them one night and set their buildings on fire and wounded one man in the leg. But the people got away from them down to the brush and Crow River.

"The Indians took all their horses and other stock and run them off. There was one dead cow found in the fort; we cleaned the fort, enlarged it and built log cabins in it. The Indians had been through all the country and had burned buildings, while at other places they had done hardly any damage. At one place there were a lot of milk cans and they punched a hole in every one, and killed all the chickens, hogs and cattle they could find. We scouted some through the country but could find no Indians. We made a lot of hay, dug a lot of potatoes and prepared for winter. We caught a badger alive. Our company was called the 'Potosi Badger Company', so we were happy. We chained him in the corner of the fort but next morning he was gone. He had got loose, slipped the strap off his head, and tore down one corner of the fort.

"On the 20th we went up on the bluff and camped, and I was detailed for fatigue duty and to report to the colonel's headquarters. The colonel gave me some matches and pointed to a large frame house and I was ordered to set fire to it, but not to go inside because it had been a smallpox hospital. It made a good fire.

"April 14th I was on provost guard duty. A boat came down the river and landed with cavalry on it. One soldier called my name from the hurricane deck. It was my brother Frank whom I had not seen for several years. He belonged to the 4th Missouri Cavalry.

"July 29th we boarded our boat again and went down the Yazoo and up the Mississippi River, reaching Lake Providence on August 1st. Here we discovered our boat to be breaking down so Companies H, B, C and F were landed. Here I was sick, lying in a tent, beginning with a fever, and no doctor along with us. Besides this, the flies and mosquitoes were so thick that there was no rest to be found. Thirty-four others were also taken sick. August 5th we were put on board another boat and taken to Vicksburg, with no care whatever—could not even get a drink of Mississippi water, for weakness.

"Arrived at Vicksburg on the 7th and was moved into a floating hospital where we received good care, but by the 14th ten comrades of the 35 were mustered out by the Great Commander. The rest of us that were well enough got on board the boat again to begin our duty once more. We got our transportation from the Provost Marshall but when we reached the boat the captain would not let us on board, so we reported to the Provost Marshall again. General Grant went to the captain of the boat and told him that he must take us to Helena, Arkansas. That was the first time I saw General Grant.

"Arrived in Helena on the 16th and found our regiment in very poor circumstances. About 2/3 of our men were sick and had been sent north to the hospital; also many had died during our absence. Out of the 100 men we had in our company, only 16 remained able to do duty. We were on picket duty nearly all the time, and I next took the ague and fever camp dysentery, which made me so sick that on August 28th, I was taken to the regiment hospital. While here I saw the man on my right, and one on my left, and the one at my feet, close their eyes in death, yet I grew better and I left the hospital September 12th under the condition that I would live on milk and crackers.

"The 20th we were three miles from Atlanta and the 21st we went back to Decatur. Here I was again put on an outpost on the morning of the 22nd. An officer came along on a horse and I stopped him and would not permit him to pass but called the captain. The stranger told the captain he was one of General Sherman's staff and that General Sherman had ordered him to come out there. At this time the captain let him pass, but I told the captain he was a Rebel spy and I think so to this very day. About 10:00 a.m. we on the outpost were relieved by Company E from Platteville and we went back half a mile and camped.

"We had picked up some blackberries and so made a blackberry pot-pie, which we ate as soon as it was done or the Rebels would have gotten it–then we got some young cabbage that I 'raised' out of somebody's garden and cooked that and some pork together. It was just about done when the picket man began firing. I took off our pork and cabbage and carried it to our tent, then fell in line of battle. Started on a run for the picket line but met the picket about halfway, with the Rebels in hot pursuit. We threw some rails into piles and got behind them and stopped them for a while, but they soon got some cannon and threw shells into the rails. How the pieces flew! We next took refuge under a large apple tree but they fired a shell at us and cut off the top of the tree and it came tearing down upon us. Next we went about 50 yards to the right to support our artillery. In this manner we each made several charges. There was but a small squad of us but we would make a charge on them and drive them back, but could not hold them and to this day I wonder that we were not all killed. We finally were compelled to fall back but one of our artillery horses would not pull so one of the men picked up a cannon ball that the enemy had fired at us and began pounding the horse's ribs. It was not long before it had charged off.

"Here is where General Ring, the officers' cook, made his gallant charge, leading his horse through the yard gate, leaving the wagon hanging on the gate post, but he and the horse going on, never missing the freight of pots and pans. But his wagon was not all that we left on the field, for here we lost some of our best men and officers, either dead or taken prisoners–about ¼ in all–and also our dish of cabbage.

"When we made our charge on the Rebels, Colonel Rusk's horse carried him too far and one Rebel caught the horse by the bridle and another caught Rusk's sword. But the colonel shot and killed the one at the horse's head and then charged back toward us; but his horse was killed on the way, falling and catching Rusk's leg under him so that he couldn't move. We made another charge and succeeded in pulling him off his horse and releasing our colonel.

"I had a hard time that day, after we reached Decatur several of us were ordered to get inside the court house, a large rock building which stood near, and shoot at the enemy from the windows. But we had only held our places about five minutes when the rebels drove our men back and got between us and them. I had always said that I would never go back to Andersonville while I could run, so about six of us started for the door.

"The Rebels called to us to surrender 'You Yankee … … …. But we did not stop. We made a swift dart through the door. Well, three of us got through, down into a small ravine along the Chattahoochee River, back of their line. We quickly turned our steps toward a little spring branch, overhung with brush, but we were quickly pursued. The two men with me were from an Ohio regiment and were unknown to me. I kept running all the time, with the Rebels following and shooting, and after running about a half mile I turned to see where my companions were and they were not to be seen, nor did I ever hear from them. I left the creek to go to our men but as soon as I did the Rebels spied me and began their firing again. I went back to the creek and ran down it about a half mile, then started up a hill. I had nearly reached the top when the enemy saw me and began firing; there were about 12 after me. I got behind a tree and gave them two shots in return, but found I had only two cartridges left so I put one of them in my gun and started on the run again.

"Ran until I got out of their sight, and traveled about three miles through the woods, then rested by a large tree. While here I heard something moving through the woods, to my right, so I got behind the tree ready to give them the best I had. It kept coming closer and I finally discerned a soldier leading a horse, but as it was getting dark I could not tell whether it was one of our soldiers or a Rebel. I halted him with my gun to my shoulder. He stopped and took the same position. I said, 'Who comes there?' He answered, 'A Union soldier.' I asked, 'Of what command?' 'Kilpatrick's Cavalry,' was the response. I asked him several other questions and finally told him to come close enough so I could see his uniform and equipment. It proved to be a Union soldier so we journeyed on together.

"We marched the 13th and 14th, reached Raleigh, North Carolina. On the 15th we marched about three miles and then got word that General Johnston had surrendered. Then the boys couldn't shout enough for they longed for home and knew that the time was not far distant when they should reach it. Went back into camp about two miles.

"The 16th was Easter Sunday and thought it the most joyful Sunday we ever had while in the army. But after so much enjoyment came the terrible news of the assassination of President Lincoln on the 17th of April. This silenced the joyous shouting of our boys; they were nearly heartbroken.

"Went into camp until the 24th, had grand review and then General Grant brought us the news that President Johnson refused to ratify the terms of General Johnston's surrender and again the next day we were ordered to move on the enemy, which we did. Marched 10 miles and then camped. About 7 o'clock in the evening our men sent up a lot of rockets to notify us that General Johnston had made a final surrender. This closed the War of the Rebellion.

"On the first of May, my birthday, we started on our homeward march. The 8th we passed through Petersburg, the 12th through Richmond in front of Libby Prison, the 16th through Fredericksburg, where General Sherman reviewed us. We reached Alexandria on the 23rd and went into camp near the Potomac River. On the 24th we crossed the Potomac into Washington and participated in the grand review. On the same day we went into camp at Crystal Springs, where we remained until the 7th of June.

"I met my brother Frank in Washington. None of we four brothers were killed during the war, but brother Frank was wounded. On June 7th we received our final muster out and started for home, arriving at Madison on June 11, 1865.

"The loss to the regiment in killed and those who died of wounds was 57; died of sickness 414, making a total of 471, which was the largest death toll of any regiment that left the state of Wisconsin. Honorable J.L. Richard, state superintendent of public instruction, at the commencement of recruiting, had authorized Lieutenant Colonel Naismith of the 25th Regiment to draw on him for $100 to be used for the benefit of the sick and wounded of the first Company raised in Grant County."

Philip wrote the following poem:

> T'was the twenty-second of July in eighteen sixty-four,
> that round the doomed Atlanta our cannon loud did roar.
> Our drums did beat to arms, and our bugles wildly blew,
> the soldiers fixed their bayonets for the signal well they knew.
>
> The Rebels rapidly advanced and soon came full in view
> with musket, sabre and the lance before our boys in blue.
> Still forward came the charging host, their courage well we knew.
> We met them as the rocky coast meets the troubled ocean blue.
>
> Our Sherman brave was in command with lips compressed he stood,
> And Logan boldly meeting there the rushing charge of Hood.
> Oh! What a charge -- the crash the yells that rent the air!

Let other pens describe the scene, but your humble band was there.

The baffled Rebels did retreat, and from the strife withdrew,
and falling back, they left the field to Sherman's "boys in blue".
And, now, long life to Sherman, and all his boys so true,
who held aloft the stars and stripes and wore the suit of blue.

Decoration Day was officially proclaimed on May 5, 1868 and first observed on May 30, 1868, shortly after the end of the American Civil War. It was first enacted to honor the Union soldiers and was celebrated near the day of reunification.

From that day forward, Philip placed the American Flag on the graves of fallen soldiers. It was Philip's hope that when he was no longer able, the tradition would continue.

"As a child, I remember going with father to all the area cemeteries to place flags on the graves of his departed comrades. He never missed being there by Memorial Day. He would be gratified to know that the area Legion Posts have continued his practice." (Source: Bertha Roesch Gibson)

By 1890 all northern states recognized the holiday. The south refused to acknowledge it and had its own separate day of honoring their Confederate soldiers. That changed after WWI when it was agreed to include American casualties of any military action. Decoration Day became Memorial Day.

———

WWI came to an end in 1918 and celebrations occurred throughout the United States. The patriotic Roesch family joined this joyous occasion as one might expect it would. Philip pulled from his old storage trunk his Civil War coat with the bullet hole in the sleeve. He dusted it off then cut it up into small pieces and passed them out as souvenirs to the cheers of family, friends and neighbors to mark the end of the war. (Philip's memoirs)

A New Generation

Philip returned to Potosi, Wisconsin after the Civil War and to his sweetheart Helen Jennette Cardey, the daughter of Russell Cardey and Mercy Ann Hampton. While waiting for Philip to return home from the war, Helen worked with the Women's Relief Corp of the Grand Army of the Republic and received a medal for her services. Three months later, on September 7, 1865 she and Philip were married, near Boice Creek in the town of Potosi at the home of the bride's parents.

Philip recalled, "It was a very rainy day and there was no bridge over the creek. It took some time and effort, but finally I managed to get across and the wedding proceeded on time."

The wedding celebrations resumed six weeks later on October 15, 1865 when Philip's sister, Regina, married Helen's brother, George Washington Cardey.

Philip purchased 80 acres of land and went into farming. From time to time he would purchase other farms until he finally had a fine farm of 357 acres.

"He was the first to bring Black Angus cattle into the state of Wisconsin. He bought them at the Chicago Livestock Show and shipped them to Potosi. While in the pen there, a cow broke out and ran down onto the marshy island bordering the Mississippi River. It was quite the show as they rounded them up." (Memoirs: Bertha Roesch Gibson.)

Besides farming, Philip was interested in local and world affairs and became a town officer in Potosi, Wisconsin. He was one of three elected to the position of supervisor for the years 1884, 1886 and 1887. (Source: History of Grant County Wisconsin, Illustrated, Copyright 1900 By C.N. Holford)

Philip continued to be extremely active in buying and selling land over a period of many years to increase not only his financial worth but security for his children as well.

Helen's parents, Russell and Mercy Cardey, were among the early pioneers of Grant County, Wisconsin. Mercy grew up among the Quakers. Her grandmother, Ann Croasdale, was a Quaker minister as was her mother. Mr. Cardey, a Republican, was born in Palmyra, New York and was a practicing Methodist. He served in the Patriot War of 1839, the failed invasion of the Canadian Rebellion. When they first settled in Potosi their nearest neighbor was one mile away, the next was seven miles away.

The family handed down a humorous story from Russell's life. "There was this bear that drove his pigs from the pen, so he shot three rifle balls into the brute. The next morning, Russell found the dead bear and brought him home. However, we hear tales that he was not the one to shoot the bear. Russell wouldn't get up in the middle of the night to see what was making the racket, so Mercy got up and fired the gun out the front door. There was no more noise so she went back to bed. The next morning the bear was found dead in the pig lot."

Russell Cardey was a man of integrity and sincerity of heart. His word was never doubted and he never did any man wrong. He was always seeking truth, by virtue of work, deed and example, striving to make a better world. Russell was a man of deep thought. He spent many quiet moments alone writing poetry.

Life's Voyage
by Russell Cardey

Children of truth of less renown
their boats commence to row
down life's small stream that ripples down
to where great waters flow.

They move along with gentle care
on the streams downward tide.
A seeking knowledge everywhere
and again the rivers side.

And embark on life's great river
the day was clear and bright.
Soon the waves roll high as ever
the clouds as dark as night.

Ah! Here some falter in the dark
that lose this star so bright.
Others press forward in their bark
towards the beacon light.

And embark on the ship Zion
that stands before the breeze.
Through the storms rage like a lion
the captain calms the seas.

Teach us our father to proclaim
thy goodness all along.
Today and yesterday the same
is our joy and our song.

The God of love is everywhere
his grace he will impart.
To all who ask with zealous care
and with a contrite heart?

Show mercy Lord 0 God forgive
our shortage in the past.
Be with us while we mortals live
and crown us thine at last.

Ah! Sweet Innocence

Ten months after Philip and Helen's marriage on July 8, 1866, their first child was born, a son, William Russell Roesch named after his maternal grandfather. A daughter, Ida Marie, was born in 1867, then Ella Josephine in 1869. Just short of seven years later, Roy Delbert arrived in 1876, then Clyde Earl in 1881. Their last and sixth child, Bertha Mae, arrived in 1883. Seventeen years had passed and their family was now complete.

Life on the farm can be a lot of fun for children. They certainly can get into a lot of mischief. Playtime can be exciting and at times downright dangerous. Philip and Helen were caring and patient parents; they were called Pa and Ma.

"While Clyde and I were playing in the hayloft one day, our little dog, Penny, climbed the 10-foot ladder trying to reach us. Clyde laid down on his stomach and reached for our dog, pulling him up the rest of the way. But, in our excitement, we leaned against the large sliding door and pushed it off the track. It went down with a loud crash. Our father couldn't see how we were able to push it off without falling with it, for which he was very thankful.

"One day after a heavy rain Clyde and I thought it would be fun to go boat riding. There was an old horse trough our father used to feed his horses when they were in the pasture. It was about six feet long and 14 inches high, made of oak and heavy as lead. It sat on top of a small hill, but, by tugging and pushing, we got it down to a small stream. Clyde got in and I pushed him off, but the 'trough turned turtle with Clyde under it'. Soon he came out and said, 'We'll have to stay down here until I get dried out so Ma won't know what happened.' It was several days before our father discovered our boat.

"One year the corn didn't come up in some places, so Pa sent Clyde and me out to 'replant those hills'. It was a very hot day and soon we tired of that job. We decided that Pa didn't know how hot it really was and finally decided

37

to just pour the seed in a pile and put a big flat rock on top. In a few days, Pa went up to see how the corn was doing.

"He told Ma 'I'd ought to have know better than to have sent those two.' But, he laughed as always.

"Clyde, eight, decided to make a bicycle using two barrel heads for wheels. He worked in the old shop all day and finally I decided to go out and see if was all set to ride yet. But, I fell down and started to cry. Mother came hurrying along to see what was the matter and Clyde said, 'She was swearing, that's why she got hurt!' I answered back, 'I was not! I was singing, *Jesus Christ, the Son of God*'.

"One day I went calling on Mrs. Morgans, taking three-year-old Mary along to play with Margaret. We heard a lot of yelling and laughter, so went in to see what it was all about. The girls were holding their fingers on the faucet and the water was spurting everywhere and dripping from the walls and ceiling. It was necessary to hang Mary's dress on the clothesline to dry before we could come home." (Source: Memoirs, Bertha Mae Roesch Gibson.) Bertha Mae was Valedictorian class of 1902, Potosi High School, Potosi, Wisconsin.

Philip and Helen's son Roy graduated with honors from Potosi High School. He went on to attend college at the Normal School at Valparaiso, Indiana. Today it is known as Valparaiso University. After graduation, he became a teaching principal at the British Hollow School in Wisconsin.

British Hollow School

Florida Bound

In 1883 Philip's oldest son, seventeen-year-old William Russell Roesch decided it was time to strike out on his own. William tells us in a personal column he wrote in the *Eau Gallie Record* on January 31, 1924 titled "A Personal Reminiscence of its Pioneer Settlers":

"I am sure you, dear reader, will pardon me if I digress a little from real Eau Gallie history in the rest of this article. I want to tell you how we got to Eau Gallie in those days, and possibly say something about conditions as I found them here and of the things that impressed me most at that time."

William recalled traveling to Le Mars, Iowa where he met up with his uncle, John McAllister, who was married to Philip's sister, Josephine. Josephine died on April 11, 1880 from childbirth complications, just 16 days after the birth of their first child, Joseph, named for her brother.

From Le Mars, they boarded the train and went south to Mobile, Alabama, then across to Jacksonville, Florida where the railroad ended.

"While in Jacksonville, we met J. E. M. Hodgson also coming to Indian River. After a short delay there waiting for the boat, we embarked on the old Frederick DeBarry for Sanford. After traveling part of the afternoon, all night and part of the next forenoon, we were landed at Sanford, a small but flourishing town.

"Here we were going to take a small boat for the upper St. Johns River, but, it had not returned from its last trip so we were compelled to wait four days for its arrival from up river.

William Russell Roesch

"It finally came, and after some necessary delays in provisioning, we were dashing up the picturesque St. Johns at the rate of nearly two miles per hour. The river was so crooked and in some places so stopped up with water lettuce, that it looked like a hopeless case.

"But all things good, bad or indifferent must come to an end, so one fine dark night the steamboat landed alongside a mule and wagon and they told us to get in as this was the Lake Poinsett landing and that it was not far to Rockledge. We joined the mule and wagon and were later landed at the Rider Hotel in Rockledge. We were traveling fast as we could; yet it was considerably more than one week since we left Jacksonville. After spending the night at the famous Rider House we embarked upon a sailboat for Eau Gallie, we had a fair wind and arrived here sometime that afternoon in the month of November of that year."

"To those who come, and those who go
we can only say that this is so.
They are today a city fair,
where we found little but balmy air."
By Wm. R. Roesch

John McAllister was originally from New Brunswick, Canada. He owned property along the Indian River in Eau Gallie and was a neighbor of John Carroll Houston III. He owned a fine orange grove and grew a large tomato garden. He was also very successful in the business of artesian well sinking. And, he was a director of the State Bank of Eau Gallie, located on the first floor of a three-story building on Highland Avenue. William H. Gleason built the building and his real estate office was on the second floor. The third floor housed the Masonic Lodge. It still stands today.

It is a well-documented fact that in 1855 Gleason, an investment banker and real estate developer from New York, moved to Wisconsin and began to develop Eau Claire, Wisconsin. When the bank smash-up occurred, he moved back to New York.

Gleason arrived in Eau Gallie, Florida with his family in 1880, which was originally named Arlington by its first setter, John Carroll Houston. In order to establish a post office, it became necessary to change the town's name because another town had already claimed the Arlington name.

It was Gleason who gave it the new name of Eau Gallie. The area has rocky ledges of coquina rock, which gives the land a firm base. Eau Gallie means rocky water. So why did Gleason select the name Eau Gallie? We find a few reasons recorded in history. One is that he named it after a river named Eau Gallie in Eau Claire, Wisconsin. Another is that Gleason took the French term eau, meaning water, and gallie, a Chippewa Indian word meaning rocky to form the name Eau Gallie.

————

It was on January 16, 1885, that the Union soldier's son, William Russell Roesch, at the age of 18, listed as a painter in that year's census, married the Confederate sympathizer's daughter, Ada Louise Houston. Ada was 27, nine years older than her new husband.

Witnesses were all Houston family members, Eugene Alexander M. Stewart, a dairy farmer, and Ada's sister, Isabel Margaret Houston Stewart, known as Belle. Belle's husband, Bethal J. Stewart, performed the marriage ceremony in Bahia and signed the certificate as Notary Public. Today Bahia is known as Palm Shores, located just north of Eau Gallie.

Ada brought into the marriage her nine-year-old daughter Eva Lena Houston. Ada was just 19 when she gave birth on May 19, 1876. William welcomed this daughter called Lena and gave her his name. Up until this time, she was listed, erroneously or perhaps deliberately, as a daughter of Ada's parents, John C. Houston III and Mary Virginia Hall. The name was originally pronounced House-ton but today, most people pronounce it as Hugh-ston.

William Russell Roesch and
Ada Louise Houston Roesch

41

Pioneer John Carroll Houston III

John Carroll Houston III was an Indian scout during the Third Seminole War. It was in the late 1850's when this pioneer arrived in Eau Gallie with a company of soldiers on an Indian hunt when the territory was just a wilderness. He fell in love with the area and decided this was where he wanted to build his home.

When the Second Seminole War ended in 1842, Congress passed the Arms Occupation Act. It gave settlers the opportunity to earn title to 160 acres by building a house, living on the land for five years and cultivating five acres. Further, that they would need to take up arms to protect themselves from the Indians that remained in Florida.

Houston returned to the fort at Enterprise, Florida and obtained a soldier's land grant for 160 acres. It encompassed all the land north of the Eau Gallie River, known as Elbow Creek, and east to the Indian River and perhaps as far west as Lake Washington. He called the area Arlington. The "official" papers for this land were dated May 20, 1862.

In 1859 with the aid of the 10 slaves his father had given him, and with his oldest sons, it took nearly a year to build the first hickory log cabin for his family. The air was heavy with mosquitoes, especially at night, so palmetto roots and green boughs were burned to keep them at bay. His plan was to cultivate the land into a pineapple and sugar cane plantation.

The few small Indian tribes that still existed in the area were not hostile to the Houstons. The Seminole exchanged animal hides and wild pork for sugar and coffee. The natives had been ordered to leave, but were reluctant to do so.

Before Houston brought his family to the East Coast, he helped his men fell sufficient logs to build the slave quarters that sat just north of their homestead. Finally, on October 5, 1860, this pioneer returned to

Enterprise for his family. His daughter Ada was three years old when her family moved. It took three weeks to drive the covered wagons hauled by oxen and the herd of cattle and horses from Enterprise to their new home. Houston, after homesteading for two years, was deeded an additional 80 acres of land by President Abraham Lincoln for his services as an Indian scout.

John's daughter Elizabeth recalls in an article printed in the *Eau Gallie Record*, Early History of Eau Gallie, 1916:

"At the time we moved to what is now Eau Gallie, our nearest store and post office was at New Smyrna, 90 miles away. Our mail and supplies were delivered, weather permitting, once a month by sailboat.

"In the spring of 1861 the War Between the States came on and our family was completely isolated. We raised all of our supplies. Corn, potatoes and beans were our staples, while the river furnished us with fish, and deer, bear and turkeys were to be had in any quantity almost in our dooryard. For salt, father built a series of evaporating troughs by hollowing out cypress logs; ocean water and sun produced all the salt needed. During the period of the war we all had to weave all the cloth we used by hand." (Source: Elizabeth Houston Sears)

The Civil War was coming to an end and Confederate Secretary of War John C. Breckenridge was a most wanted war criminal with a high priority for capture dead or alive. He, along with his entourage, was trying to escape capture by Union forces. While sailing down the Indian River attempting to reach Cuba his boat sprung a leak. He came ashore seeking assistance at Houston's dock. John helped him caulk his boat so that Breckenridge could continue his successful escape.

It was in 1862 when Abraham Lincoln signed the Emancipation Proclamation ending slavery. But real freedom did not come until the Confederacy conceded to the Union and the ratification of the Thirteenth Amendment was signed prohibiting slavery, freeing approximately 4,000 slaves. An attempt was made to ship all former slaves to a colony outside the country. Houston's slave quarters now sat empty.

In 1864, Houston began serving as the Brevard County commissioner and did so for a period of 10 years. On June

John Carroll Houston III

43

20, 1871 he was named the first postmaster of Eau Gallie, Brevard County, Florida. John signed the contract as postmaster July 9, 1871.

According to the agriculture census dated June 30, 1885, Houston had a total of 15 acres tilled, three acres of pasture and 100 acres of woodland. Sweet potato was planted on 1/4 of an acre, and on another 1/4 acre he grew pineapples. He had 100 orange trees growing on three acres, all bearing fruit. He grew rice and oxen powered his sugar cane mill. There was three acres of pasture for his 20 barnyard animals. His salt mine was just south of their home. (Source: Ancestry.com)

Houston's father, John Carroll Houston II, lived on Talbot Island near the mouth of the St. John's River. He and his brother, Major Samuel Houston, had left North Carolina at the same time. John Houston II went to north Florida and the Major and his family went to Tennessee. The Major's son, the famous General Sam Houston of Texas, became a great friend of the Indians west of the Tennessee River and was adopted by Chief Oolooteka who was the leader of the Cherokee people.

There is controversy over the relationship of Houston and General Houston by genealogists. However, the family remains steadfast in its convictions.

The relationship to General Samuel Houston of Texas fame goes as follows:

Robert Houston had two sons, John Carroll and Major Samuel Houston. John Carroll went to Talbot Island, Florida and his brother, Major Samuel Houston, went to Tennessee. The Major had a son, General Samuel Houston. He was a nephew to the Major's brother, John Carroll Houston. (Source: Jessie Stewart, great granddaughter of J. C. Houston III)

We know that John Carroll Houston III and his cousin General Samuel Houston had at least one thing in common. Sam made his way to Texas, making friends with the Cherokee Indians, and John Houston III traveled into the wilderness of the Indian River country, making friends with the Seminoles. He learned the language well. Once, the General ventured to Florida for a visit with his cousin.

John gave some of his surrounding 80 acres of land in Eau Gallie to his children. His daughter Mary Houston married Charles J. Young who came to Eau Gallie in 1884 and worked at the sawmill. Mary gave away her dower of land for the St. John's Episcopal Church to be built. The couple then signed the warranty deed completing the lot transfer. (Witness, Henry Hodgson and JNO. E. M. Hodgson, Notary Public, deed Book "B.B." pg. 650, May 1, 1897.)

They assisted by money and work in building St. John's with the help of others. The street, on which the church was built, Young Street, was named for her. They were among the first 29 communicants.

John C. Houston III donated the land in front of his home for a road that is named for him, Houston Street. Up until then the house just sat in the woods.

In the nineteenth century it was common to bury family members on their own property. The Pioneer Houston Family Cemetery sits within eyesight of the slaves' quarters. The first family member laid to rest was John's son, 27-year-old Samuel, who died February 17, 1883 of typhoid fever. The deceased was laid out on a cooling board in the parlor for viewing so relatives and friends could pay their final respects. It was customary, during this era, for family members to sit up all night with the body. "The old cooling board was kept at the local lumber house." (Source: Sue Stewart Seawright and Mamie Clifford Houston Carter)

There are a total of 22 family members buried in the Houston cemetery that sits among the palm and oak trees. Unfortunately, vandalism hit in 1992 with a vengeance. Some of the gravestones were smashed, and others were allegedly thrown down the riverbank and into the water. A $250 reward for the return of the missing stones was offered. None as of this date have ever surfaced. Today we know the names of only 12 that rest here.

It was in 1910 that the City of Eau Gallie would not permit any more Houston family members to be buried there. It certainly must have been a difficult and certainly a sad situation for the families to accept, because husbands could not be laid to rest next to their wives and parents could not be buried with their babies. It was decreed that all future burials must be in the Eau Gallie Cemetery that had been established in 1902. The cemetery is located on Masterson Street, off U.S. Route 1.

William R. Roesch was recorded as owning 200 acres. Part of this land was the dower Ada gave to her husband providing a good financial beginning. To begin their life together the newlyweds moved into the house that was originally built for the slaves' quarters to which he built a comfortable addition. All homes during this period had fences around their properties to keep their farm animals in and the neighbors' animals out.

Ada's father died November 22, 1885, 10 months after she married, leaving 160 acres. William filed a claim for this tract of land that the act of Congress had officially approved for Houston back on May 20, 1862, some 23 years earlier, and proceeded to build two homes. However, a dispute arose and construction came to a halt until the government land authorities settled the case. Although William claimed ownership to the land, the official document was not signed and dated until the fifth day of February 1896, almost 11 years after Houston's death. The document reads:

The United States of America

To All To Whom These Presents Shall Come, Greeting:
Now know ye, *That there is therefore granted by the* **UNITED STATES** *unto the said* **William R. Roesch** **TO HAVE AND TO HOLD** *the said tract of Land, with the appurtenances thereof, unto the said* **William R. Roesch** *and to his heirs and assigns forever. In testimony where of I,* **Grover Cleveland,** *President of the United States of America, have caused these letters to be made Patent, and the Seal of the General Land Office to be hereunto affixed.*

William was running an established business, the Wm. R Roesch, Dealer in Hay, Grain, Cotton, Seed, Meal, and Fertilizers. But, not long after the dispute was settled, William wrote a letter dated Feb 19, 1897 on his business stationery addressed to the Honorable W. H. H. Gleason explaining he was closing his business, and that there was an amount of between $250 and $300 left on his books, and that he would like to assign these accounts to him. Mr. Roesch explained, "that there would be little trouble to collect" and he offered to pay the "usual commission", or he would take a "good business lot", and he, Gleason, could keep what he collects. (Source: Copy of letter provided by the Florida Historical Society)

Taken Prisoner

Ada's brother, John C. Houston IV, was born April 3, 1842 at Mayport, Florida where he resided until the age of seven. Then his parents moved to Enterprise, Florida, which was deemed the most "most civilized town in the state". From here, young John moved to Jacksonville where he resided with his grandmother and went to school.

At the outbreak of the Seminole Indian War in 1857, he enlisted in the U.S. Army as a scout at the age of 16. He served for two years. It was when he returned from the war, that he and his father moved to Eau Gallie, then named Arlington, in 1859, and together built a log home in the middle of the woods for the family.

From 1860 to 1865, at the outbreak of the Civil War, John IV began to operate boats on the Indian River in the interest of the Confederacy. In fact, he was the first man to navigate this river and became known as Captain John. He made several successful trips to Nassau, British West Indies transporting provisions. He was captured, taken prisoner and kept at sea for three months. At the end of the Civil War Captain John was paroled at Key West.

"He worked his way up on the island until he reached what was then called the Town of Miami. He got an old hunter to ferry him across the river onto the peninsula. The Captain, armed only with a small hatchet, made his way toward Eau Gallie. The journey back was fraught with danger as he was encountered at frequent intervals with panther and other wild animals. When he reached Jupiter, he found a dilapidated old boat and with his hatchet and an old saw blade that was lying nearby he built a small boat and paddle and headed home up the river."

His parents thought their son was surely dead. But, one night at midnight his father awoke to the call of a "cow-holler". He jumped out of bed yelling to his wife that their son was home because no one else could holler like that. John ran toward the river to joyfully welcome his son home.

Captain John fell in love and married Susan Elizabeth Stewart of LaGrange, Florida on September 5, 1860 and brought her to Eau Gallie to live. Just as his father, he too served as county commissioner from 1894 to 1900. He died at his home in Eau Gallie on Tuesday, February 22, 1916, after a long and lingering illness. His pallbearers were J.F.M. Hodgson, C. L. Taylor, A. N. Mathers, J. T. Snell, Thomas Hutto Braddock and James W. Rossetter. He was buried in the Eau Gallie Cemetery.

(The foregoing information was gathered in part by Jessie Stewart and from the February 25, 1916 *Eau Gallie Record*, obituary, written by William Russell Roesch, Capt. Houston Called After A Long Illness, Was The Oldest Resident of Eau Gallie, and includes excerpts from the memoirs of the late Jessie Stewart, titled "The Settling of Eau Gallie and Early Life on the Indian River".)

Early Stewart Family History

The Stewart, Houston and Roesch families were connected through the marriage of Captain John Houston IV and Susan Elizabeth Stewart. William, who married Houston's sister, Ada, offers us an early Stewart family lineage in his *Eau Gallie Record* column:

A Personal Reminiscence of its Pioneer Settlers

"About 1863 Johnathan Stewart moved his family to a place about one fourth mile south of Horse Creek and two miles north of Elbow Creek. Mr. Stewart was a farmer and came originally from Hamilton County in this state, though he had lived at what is now LaGrange, then called Sand Point, for a number of years. Mr. Stewart brought a large family of children with him, who all settled in this immediate vicinity, as follows: Mary M., who later became Mrs. John L. Casper; James T. Stewart, who made a fine home on the island, later moving to Delray where he died some years ago; Susan E., who later became the wife of Capt. John Houston; Emma E., who married Gardner S. Hardee and made her home at Rockledge; Charles L. Stewart, who still lives about one mile west of Eau Gallie, and Anna L. who became the wife of Robert Charles Creech, later removing to West Palm Beach. Johnathan Stewart and his wife Elizabeth are both buried on the old homestead. Of the children, only two, Charles L. Stewart and Mrs. R. C. Creech are now living."

Rutherford B. Hayes was President of the United States when Homestead Certificate No. 1142 was issued to Johnathan R. Stewart for 94 and 50/100ths acres of land.

Johnathan and his wife were initially buried on their land and later were reverently moved to the family plot in the Eau Gallie Cemetery.

Governor William H. Gleason

William H. Gleason was elected lieutenant governor, and while serving proclaimed himself governor of Florida when the Legislature adjourned and the Senate was debating the impeachment of the sitting governor, Harrison Reed. When the State Adjutant General and the sheriff sided with Reed, they surrounded the governor's office to prevent Gleason from occupying the space.

Governor Reed charged Gleason with being ineligible for public office whereas he had not been a resident of the state for the mandated three years. On December 14, 1868 Gleason was forced from office. He moved to Dade County and served in the Florida House of Representatives from 1871 to 1874.

Gleason moved back to Eau Gallie from Biscayne Bay, Dade County, Florida in the fall of 1882. (Source: Mrs. George (Elizabeth) W. Sears, *Eau Gallie Record* column, Early History of Eau Gallie)

Gleason is listed in the 1885 census as having 5,000 acres of woodland. At a later date we see him with 16,000 acres.

"At this time Gleason started to plat Section 16 and he laid it all out in two lots. He at that time was engaged with his brother-in-law, a Mr. Carpenter, in the erection of a sawmill on Elbow Creek. These enterprises attracted some attention in the sparsely settled section of the county and gave Eau Gallie its first start as a community."

(Source: William Russell Roesch, *Eau Gallie Record* column 1916, Early History of Eau Gallie)

Faith and Family

A house of worship for all faiths in this new community had not yet materialized. The Baptists built a church on Highland Avenue in 1888 and they were more than willing to permit use of their building to the Methodists when they were not occupying it. The Bible gave hope and inspiration in a desolate and unknown land.

In 1890 William R. Roesch and his wife Ada, along with all the followers of Methodism, met under the supervision of William for Sunday school. On those occasions, when a guest minister was not available, William would prepare and give the sermon. From the years 1890 to 1900, worshipers met any and everywhere they could find space.

St. Paul's Methodist Church, Eau Gallie, Fl.
Photo from The Pulse circa 1900

In 1900, a formal organization was created and William and Ada were among the first few to sign the charter. It was with faith and vision that this small group undertook the building of St. Paul's Methodist Church. The first service was held in 1902. J. B. Hawk became the first resident pastor. (Source: *The Pulse*, St. Paul's Methodist Church)

Sadly, this first old sanctuary burned down on Friday, August 6, 1965 following the junior M.Y.F. skit coincidently entitled "Four Ways the Church Could Fall Down". The church was rebuilt and continues to serve the community to this day. (Source: *The Pulse*, of Saint Paul's United Methodist Church of Eau Gallie, Florida)

Ada gave her husband a precious gift, a Bible, The Oxford Self Promoting Bible, S.S. Teacher Edition. It reads, "W. R. Roesch 1904 a present from Ada L. Roesch". This Bible has been passed down through the generations. An elderly, feeble William, with hand shaking, signed his name passing it on to his stepdaughter, writing simply, "Given to Lena (Roesch) Dean." It was then passed to his grandson, Lena's nephew, with the notation, "Given to Russell Roesch in 1942–in mother's care (Florence) presented to him Jan. 1, 1957". Next, it was passed on to Russell's sister, William's granddaughter, "Given to Elsie Roesch Smith on March 19, 2008 to be passed on to Kathryn Smith Lockhard". Elsie then passed this gift on to her daughter, "Given to Kathryn Smith Lockhard on March 23, 2008". The Bible remains, as of this writing, in her care, the great granddaughter of William R. Roesch. Cut out and glued onto this page in the Bible was the newspaper article of the 62nd wedding anniversary of William's parents, Philip and Helen.

Inside the Bible there are many bookmarks indicating various versus. A faded Fifth Premium ribbon from the Lenawee County Fair Association, State of Michigan, lay inside. The fair started in 1839 and continues today. There was also a white ribbon with red lettering for an Epworth League Convention, held in Deland, Florida, Jacksonville District, October 12-13 in 1904 that Lena attended. Postmarked 1941 from Cocoa, Florida is a Christmas card addressed to Lena, signed by "Scott, Florence and Kiddies".

Heartbreak, Happiness and Home

William and Ada's first child, a daughter, Mary, was born December 22, 1885 named for Ada's mother. What a special Christmas gift. The joy would turn to heartbreak, however, when Mary died on May 2, 1887. Just 30 days prior, they suffered the loss of their newborn son who was born on April 2, 1887 and died the very next day. Painful tragedies continued to plague Ada and William. A daughter was stillborn on January 15, 1888 and then on August 22, 1889 another daughter was stillborn. Ada gave birth on May 2, 1893 to their second son, and fifth baby, William Phillip, named after his father and grandfather. Their prayers had been answered. They called him Willy.

Roesch Babies – Houston Family Pioneer Cemetery

Ada gave birth one last time, at the age of 38, to a son, Earl Leroy, born on October 7, 1895, who left this earth on October 25, 1895. All five babies are buried together in the Houston family cemetery on Highland Avenue.

In May of 1901, William began to build a fine new home for his family on a very choice site of land he owned on the corner of Highland Avenue and Old Oak Street, just across the street from the old original slave quarters where they were living. June 14 arrived and now William was really pushing hard every day to complete his house as fast as possible. (Source: *Florida Star*, Titusville)

It was and is architecturally significant as a fine example of turn-of-the-century frame vernacular style house that features fish scale ornamentation and shiplap siding. Details include a tin roof, and two over two double-hung sash windows. It is a two-story home with four bedrooms on the second floor. Finally, on June 28, 1901 they were able to move in.

William and Ada often invited Rev. Hawk over for Sunday dinner. Children during this era were to be seen and not heard. So when the minister was a guest, their son Willy ate his dinner after the guest had left. However, it was not unusual for Ada to sneak her son a piece of chicken. (Source: Clyde Wilson Roesch)

Roesch House on Highland Avenue (Photo 2009)

William subdivided his land and built homes, known as The Roesch Cottages. Both sides of the entire length of the street were lined with big beautiful oak trees. They were gracefully draped with Spanish moss forming a cool shadowy archway over the road. He also built a cottage that sat behind his home on Old Oak Street.

Celebrations and Tragedies

On January 28, 1887 Mathias Eugene Roesch died of pneumonia at the age of 74 years, 11 months and 10 days. He was laid to rest in Boice Creek Cemetery in Potosi, Wisconsin near his farmhouse. His life on earth had come to an end, but his dream lives on through future generations, because he brought his family to America for a better life.

An administrator's sale took place 10 months later on October 13, 1887, on his farm on Boice Creek, in the town of Potosi, to sell at public auction commencing at 10 a.m. the following: "Eight Cows, 2 three-year old Heifers, 2 two-year-old Heifers, 2 three-year-old Steers, 3 two-year-old Steers, 9 yearlings, and 6 calves. Farm machinery includes a horse rake, corn plow, wagon, seeder and fanning mill."

The funds raised from the auction enabled his wife Julia to care for their home and youngest sons still living at home, thirteen-year-old August and fifteen-year-old Otto. The last person known to live in the homestead was Louis, son of Mathias and Julia.

THE OLDEST HOME ON BOICE CREEK
Old Mathias Roesch Homestead
By H. E. Roethe

"At a bend in the road, where the ground was miry and wet from a lovely spring, and not visible until you come right to it, we came across it, in one of our wanderings down the hollow below the schoolhouse and the old mill, the oldest house on Boice Creek. It struck our fancy, the tiny, unpretentious porch in front, the old clapboards, the two roof windows in the roof that was scarcely slanting, the picket fence that had seen its best days, the shingles that had been made in the home kitchen, at night and during spare time, by hand, from blocks of wood cut from a tree on the place, how we longed for a

Kodak to take a picture of it, so as to have something for recollection when "the old gives place to the new", and the time-worn and time-honored pioneer structure, inhabited until now, is succeeded by the more pretentious dwelling at its side on a more elevated site. But other people have cameras, and to them we are indebted for a fine picture of the old Mathias Roesch homestead, and from which the accompanying cut in the Times was made. Few of these old homes are left, and in all probability they will not be standing for many more years."

———

Philip and Helen were well known and respected in the community. They were a sociable couple and had made many friends and acquaintances throughout the years. Philip had become successful and accomplished and was able to retire to his farm in Potosi not long after his father's death.

On February 1, 1888 a special celebration occurred. Philip and Helen's daughters, Ida and Ella, were married in a double ring ceremony in their Victorian style parlor. The brides wore gracefully flowing high-waisted full-length white silk and lace gowns with yoke necklines, a popular design during this era. Their modest sheer veils would have just kissed their fingertips. The sisters would have carried a single red rose to mark their romantic Valentine wedding. Together, they were escorted into the parlor on the arms of their very proud "Pa."

"Mr. Henry Korber married Miss Ida M. Roesch and one minute later Mr. William L. Gelbach was tied to Miss Ella J. Roesch. Mr. and Mrs. Roesch took the mingled loss and blessing as well as could be expected. Rev. E. M. Corey tied the two knots up quick and in the most approved fashion. The parents were congratulated on the addition of two fine sons-in-law."

"The men had made a most excellent selection for their companions in life. The husbands, on the other hand, were thrifty, energetic businessmen, and neither of the men, smoked, chewed, nor drank." (Source: *The Oshkosh Northwestern*, Oshkosh, Wisconsin)

Quiet Slumber

"It was early evening on the 30th of July 1895. Philip and Helen's son, Roy, attended the young people's summer camp. Here you could enjoy all the pastimes of fishing, wading, swimming and cycle riding. Roy had on his bathing suit and was in the company of Mr. Kolb, principal of the Potosi High School.

"They concluded they would swim across the deep channel down to the camp instead of walking around the rough riprap and hot sand along the shore. Mr. Kolb swam off and into the deep water. Roy went boldly to near the center of the dam and jumped in where the water proved to be twenty feet deep or more.

"Roy, not the strongest of swimmers, lost his courage and became frightened. Roy cried out for help as he kept slipping under the water. Mr. Kolb was nearly within reach when Roy went under for the last time. Two fishermen hearing the cries for help brought a skiff and rope with a grappling hook attached, but they were too late.

"In one brief hour, he who had been the life and soul of the camp, the joy and pride of all hearts, a most exemplary young man in town was laying there before them. Roy was dead at the age of 18 years, 11 months and 12 days.

"At four o'clock in the morning the body was conveyed to the desolate home of his heart-broken parents, Philip and Helen Roesch. The burial service was at the house on Thursday afternoon and burial followed at the British Hollow Cemetery. The family and friends that accompanied the remains to the grave was the largest ever seen in recent times. Appropriate remarks were made at the gravesite and there was singing by the church choir of which Roy was a member.

"A young man in the strength and beauty of his days had fallen among them, a life full of promise and usefulness had been extinguished, and a deep sorrow fell upon the people. Peace, to his quiet slumber, and gently distill the dews in heaven over his early grave."

It was further noted in his obituary "Roy graduated with much honor from the Potosi High School in 1893. The next fall and winter he attended the Normal School (Valparaiso University) at Valparaiso, Indiana, and the next winter taught and was principal of the British Hollow School. He was retained for the ensuing year for the same position at the time of his death." (Source: *Grant County Herald*, Lancaster, Wisconsin)

Roy Delbert Roesch

Fun, Frolic and Fishing

Winter was fast approaching in Lancaster, Wisconsin, so Philip and Helen headed south to Eau Gallie, Florida. They purchased a two-story wooden frame cottage that their son William built next door to his home on December 21, 1912 for the sum of one dollar and other valuable consideration. (Source: Quite-claim-deed)

It was a comfortable dwelling with a brick fireplace in the living room, good to take the chill out of ones bones on a cool morning or evening. In front of Philip's home was a beautiful lanky oak tree laced with Spanish moss. He and his wife would sit in the shade of this tree on any given day and enjoy the cool breezes that whispered up from the Indian River.

Philip and Helen's winter cottage on Highland Street
Just to the left is the Wm. R. Roesch House (photo 2008)

William's brother Clyde and his wife, Julia Keehner, purchased the house next door to his parents in 1925. Julia was a lady in every sense of the word. She just loved to have her tea in floral teacups and she taught kindergarten in Sunday school. They both enjoyed the winter months in sunny Eau Gallie. (Source: Elsie Louise Roesch Smith)

Many times you would see Philip hanging onto his fishing pole as if it were a trophy. He and his sons, William and Clyde, were often seen happily fishing in various spots along the fish packed Indian River.

Philip with Fishing Pole in Hand

William snapped a picture of his proud and happy father and brother, somewhat boastful, after the two returned home from one of their many fishing excursions. The photo is testimony as to how plentiful the river really was. One picture was made into a postcard that Philip mailed to his family and friends who were still braving the blustery winter cold back in Wisconsin.

One such postcard was sent to Philip's youngest brother, John Albert. On the back of the card it reads: "Catch, Feb 2, 1915. Talking about sport reminds us of a small catch of fish made Tuesday of this week by Phil and Clyde Roesch. In two hours trolling these two gentlemen landed forty-three trout, all good-sized ones and had many more 'strikes' that would not stick. These fish were all caught within a half-mile of the city wharf." The forgoing was typed on the post card and then hand written is this: "Fine weather. All Well. Come and catch a few."

Clyde and his father Philip with fish caught in the Indian River
Picture taken February 2, 1915

This was a great time for the family to be together and many wonderful memories were created. William rarely made it to family reunions back home in Lancaster, Wisconsin due to his many civic responsibilities. Here we see these visits publicized.

Eau Gallie Record

April 16, 1925

Mr. and Mrs. Phil Roesch left for their home in
Lancaster, Wisconsin on Tuesday last. They were fortunate
in being able to take the Dixie Flyer from this place direct
to Chicago without change. The condition of Mrs. Roesch's
health caused them to return earlier than usual this year.

Also on April 16, 1925

Mr. and Mrs. Clyde E. Roesch left via auto for their
home in Potosi, Wisconsin this morning. Mr. Roesch is
conceded to be Eau Gallie's champion fisherman and it is not ·
hard to believe that those bass, sergeant and trout are glad
that he has gone. While here, he purchased and fitted up a
nice home to which they will return in the early fall.

Three months after returning to Potosi, Clyde and Julia gave birth to their first and only child, a son, Walter Christian Roesch, born August 9, 1925.

Walter, who took music lessons, could be seen as a young boy carrying his violin to school. As an adult he played the piano. He also played the organ in his church in Potosi, Wisconsin. (Source: Elsie Louise Roesch Smith)

Passing Judgment

William Russell Roesch

William R. Roesch was becoming more and more involved with community affairs. He did a little land surveying, not for money, more like a civic donation to community and friends. He was well respected in his hometown of Eau Gallie, Florida and in 1887 he was elected its first town treasurer. He also became a notary public and in this capacity performed many marriages over the years.

In 1892 William was part of the Brevard County Reform Association, which became involved in controversy over county finances, particularly the county commission's expenditure of $8,000 on the county jail and resulting treasury deficit.

The controversy, personal at times and chronicled in *History of Brevard County* Volume 1, written by Herrell H. Shoener, and sponsored by the Brevard

County Historical Commission, raged into the next year and the reform group was asked to support a resolution condemning county commissioner Cornthwaite J. Hector. The group wanted E. G. Vivell appointed in his place.

A meeting was held in the Eureka Hotel in Eau Gallie. William Roesch and others joined John Aspinwall, the major speaker. The resolution of condemnation was adopted, but the new Florida governor, Henry Mitchell, urged instead a harmonious truce between the factions, and Hector was retained.

William Roesch followed in the heels of his father-in-law, John C. Houston III. He was named county commissioner of District No. 5, Eau Gallie on March 9, 1905 term to expire January, 1909. He was appointed postmaster, first by President Woodrow Wilson in 1913-1917 then again in 1918-1920. President Warren Harding appointed him to the post again in 1921-1922, serving for a total of nine years.

In 1907 William R. Roesch started a newspaper, the *Eau Gallie Record*, and was its publisher and editor. His son, William Phillip, now age 14, would join his father after school to learn the publishing business.

Two years later, on April 23, 1909 William ceased publication.

"Editor Roesch got out a good local paper and made a brave effort in the nearly two years' time he managed the *Record* so well. And, if Brevard County hadn't already been overworked in the newspaper business, he would probably have met with the success that he well merited. Five weekly papers in a county with less than 4000 population is entirely too much. There isn't a county in the state that can put up such a showing." (Source: The *Florida Star*, Titusville)

However, once ink runs through the veins of an editor, it never dies. The *Eau Gallie Record* was reborn around 1916. It is in these newspapers that we occasionally find stories of William and his family.

William Russell Roesch was the first elected mayor of Eau Gallie in 1896. The term was for one year and council set salary. The position was one with broad powers that included sitting as the city judge and if there was an ordinance he didn't approve of, he could reject it. From that day forward he would be called "The Judge". Even today, when old families of Eau Gallie speak of those days in history, William is still referred to in this fashion. As the town grew, William found the need to retire from the newspaper to devote more time as mayor. His son took over the responsibility of the *Record* and proved that he too was an entrepreneur.

As mayor, William presided over the Mayor's Court, and here we read about one of his cases that was printed in the *Eau Gallie Record*.

Three Negroes Fined In
Mayor's Court Monday
Feb. 19, 1925

Chief of Police Fraser was on the job Saturday night and had five, all Negros, lined up for the Mayor's attention Monday morning. Charlie Robbins, disorderly conduct $10.00 and cost. T. J. Catchings, traffic violation and possession of liquor $50.00 and cost. M. L. Frazier, traffic violation, $10.00 and cost. Two companions of the same last name were discharged.

It was during his third term of office that the young village of Eau Gallie, spurred by a highly active Chamber of Commerce, experienced rapid growth, not only residentially, but also commercially. The Judge had the ability to lead with an authoritative, soft-spoken voice that was not easily challenged. It was a time when new bridges were authorized across the Indian and Eau Gallie Rivers, and when a new railroad depot was planned for the corner of Cypress and Fifth Streets.

Jess E. Karrick, familiarly called Jessee, was the owner of a fine grocery store he built in 1918 right on Highland Avenue. The building was 16 x 39 feet with an inventory value of $800. Sugar was selling at .28 a lb. and butter sold for .60 a lb. He became the first fire chief in town because his store was conveniently located directly across the street from the fire station.

The Judge became a volunteer fireman and he counted Jessee as one of a close-knit circle of good friends, all of whom took an active interest in the growing community of Eau Gallie. The fire station was in a building that also housed the Police Department and City Hall. Whenever there was a fire, a siren that sat on the very top of the third floor would sound the alarm to call in William and all the other local volunteers. These men would arrive at the station on Highland Avenue and would push the fire truck out of the station. Chief Karrick tells about the first pumper that was purchased on August 11, 1916, and mounted on a trailer.

"If a car could not be found, the men walked or pulled the trailer," Chief Karrick said. "It seldom made it. One time the fire truck overturned in Horse Creek. Another time it fell into Elbow Creek and it burned one time. Actually, the hand bucket brigade did a better job." (Source: Blue historical markers)

Ernest B. Taylor was also among William's close-knit friends in the community. He too was a volunteer fireman and also held the position of road supervisor. In this capacity he announced in the *Eau Gallie Record*, "the grading and paving of Pineapple Avenue was nearing completion and the roadway will be one of the most desirable streets in town."

Pineapple Avenue is lined with palm and shady oak trees that run parallel with the Indian River. Those fortunate enough to live in one of the homes that line the river's edge enjoy its splendid beauty as the sunlight sparkles down upon the surface glistening as diamonds dancing upon the blue salt water. The varying degrees of pink, red, purple and orange sunrises are spectacular. Witnessed are manatees munching sea grasses around the wood planked boat docks and dolphins appear to race as they dive and resurface repeatedly. Then there are the threatening dark and stormy days when the river is gray and choppy with white caps as lightening streaks across the sky and the sea life is quiet.

William loved everything about Eau Gallie and each evening as dusk began to descend he would light the lanterns that sat upon the posts throughout the town.

The town's first school where young Willy attended classes sits on the west side of Pineapple Avenue. William H. Gleason's home built around 1892 is here too on the west side and is listed on the National Register of Historic Places. Today this Victorian style home is a three-story bed and breakfast known as The Old Pineapple Inn. Each suite is named after a Gleason family member.

In 1924 William R. Roesch wrote, "The writer has made his home here since 1883 with varied degrees of success in a financial way, but always looking forward to the time when Eau Gallie would become one of the foremost cities of the east coast."

The Judge took whatever steps he deemed necessary to make Eau Gallie the best it could be.

PROCLAMATION BY THE MAYOR
To the People of the city of Eau Gallie

Whereas the city is making a special effort to keep all streets and alleys in a clean, presentable and sanitary condition, and much labor and effort is being expended in that direction, and as there is considerable private property within the city limits that is in a more or less unsanitary condition by reason of accumulation of trash and growth of obnoxious weeds and brush and other unsanitary conditions which constitutes a real menace to health as well as giving the city a very objectionable appearance and being a great detriment to the city generally.

Therefore, it becomes necessary to provide for the systematic abatement of all such menacing conditions, and I as Mayor of the City do hereby call upon each and every property owner or tenant, asking for your hearty support and cooperation in a real clean up campaign in the city and for that purpose do designate the week beginning July 27th and ending August 14, 1925 as **clean-up-week**, *and I respectfully request that all property, whether occupied or unoccupied be placed in a good clean, sanitary condition before the 3rd day of August, 1925. I further ask your continued effort to at all times have a clean city.*

An inspection of all property will be made August 3rd, 1925, and if any is found to be in an unsanitary or objectionable condition, the owners or tenants will be held responsible, and will be proceeded against as by ordinance provided. All sanitary ordinances will be rigidly enforced.

Dated this 10th day of July, A. D. 1925,
Wm. *R. ROESCH,*
Mayor, City of Eau Gallie, Fla.

Passage of Time

One of the few times we see Willy as a child he is with his parents, William and Ada, as guests attending the wedding of Miss Isabelle M. Hopkins and Mr. Alfred P. Chambliss. This marriage, held on Wednesday, June 24, 1903, was the very first ceremony held at the St. John's Episcopal Church on Young Street in Eau Gallie.

In the early 1870's Dr. George W. Holmes was the first physician to practice medicine in Brevard County. He set up his practice on the river in City Point, a small village north of Eau Gallie that sat between Cocoa and Sharpes, so that he could quickly sail north or south to take care of his patients. He charged $2 a call or $1 a mile.

"Dr. Holmes was a fine man, always jolly. He often told me that my father, (Captain John C Houston IV) taught him to smoke a pipe. He said he was on the boat with father and the wind was blowing hard. As fast as father would strike a match, the wind would blow it out, so father asked the doctor to hold the tiller for him, and father went to the bow of the boat, got under the deck and lit his pipe. Doctor said anything that was that much trouble to anyone must give them a lot of pleasure, so the next time he got where he could get a pipe, he bought one and started smoking." (Source: Laura Houston Braddock)

One day Willy took a bad fall and broke his left leg. The only way to get word that medical treatment was needed was to tell the steamboat captain to please relay the information up river until it eventually reached Dr. Holmes. This leg injury plus a slight spinal curve would later disqualify him from serving in the military.

Willy spent a lot of time as a young lad with his father at the newspaper learning the business. Gradually over the years he gained the knowledge and experience required to finally assume the responsibility of publishing the paper and writing his own editorials.

Willy the little boy became a man called Bill. His draft card describes him with fair complexion, 5 feet, 11 and 3/4 inches tall with brown hair, blue eyes and weighed 165 pounds.

Bill's son Clyde tells how his father loved hunting. "My father taught me how to hunt deer with a 12 gage shotgun using double ought (OO) buckshot without missing his target and wasting a shell. Dad especially enjoyed hunting with his favorite Uncle Clyde. On one of their hunting trips, the two flushed out some deer. The deer came running out single file in front of Clyde and he killed five with five shots. Pretty good shooting or at least a good-story telling. Dad also enjoyed fishing, gardening and horseback riding. All these outdoor activities later gave him a ruddy complexion."

Bill was a faithful member of the Masonic Lodge. He was a soft-spoken man, a Roesch trait, but he also spoke only when absolutely necessary and with as few words as possible. But, he proved that his pen, at least, was mightier than the sword. He was also ambitious. Bill ventured into other income producing arenas as seen by this advertisement that the *Record* also did commercial printing.

The Eau Gallie Record, 1921
"We cater to commercial printing backed by quality, and over many years' experience enables us to give the very, very best in printing. Send us your next order for printing."
Eau Gallie Record
Eau Gallie, Florida

He had a quick wit about him and he never refrained from writing exactly what he wanted to say. In a May 26, 1921 editorial, William P. Roesch wrote under the heading:

The Way of the World
The editor goes on week after week boosting the town and community and advocating the doctrine of trading at home. The local businessman pats the editor on the back and says—that's the right idea; tell it to 'em. He then refuses to help support the paper with his advertising and calmly sends an order to an out-of-town print shop for a supply of stationery. Funny world, isn't it?

He even told personal stories exhibiting his dry sense of humor.

August 27, 1925
Rattlesnake Pays Call
At Editor's Home
Last Thursday afternoon a five foot rattlesnake sporting 5 rattles,
a button and an evil disposition was discovered emerging from
under the house on Highland Avenue near Montreal, occupied
by the editor of the Record. The snake was killed but the editor
is now walking on tiptoe and staying home nights.

It was also learned that W.P. Roesch was an insurance agent. The following ad appeared:

Don't Wait Until The Fire
Alarm is Sounded
Insure
Your Property Today and Let The Other Fellow
Do The Worrying
Strong, Reliable Companies
Represented by
W.P. Roesch, Agent

Plans were underway for expansion. It was announced in the *Melbourne Times*, September 3, 1924:

W. P. Roesch, manager of the Record Printing Company and
publisher of the Eau Gallie Record, announced today that his
company had completed arrangements whereby they would
immediately undertake the publication of a weekly newspaper
at Sebastian. The first issue of the newspaper is scheduled to
make its appearance on September 12, and has the full support
of Sebastian's recently organized Chamber of Commerce.

Mr. Roesch will be in direct charge of the paper and will
announce the name of the publication together with the name
of the local editor later in the week.

There was also an announcement by W.P. Roesch, publisher, that there would soon be "*The Brevard County Developer*, a monthly magazine to appear on March 20, 1925, illustrated with pictures showing the county's progress."

Bill and Nellie Forever

William would occasionally make the trek from Florida to Wisconsin with his wife Ada and their two children, Lena and Willy, to visit family. These visits were too far and few between, but always a joyous occasion. Young Willy loved the long trip to see his grandparents, Philip and Helen, at their farmhouse. His aunts and uncles always extolled a lot of attention on him because they didn't get to see him very often. Plus there were numerous cousins to play with so he was never bored.

Come Sunday, playtime was set aside. The children went to Sunday school as the adults attended church services. Willy knew some of the children for their parents were friends of the family. One of these children was a girl by the name of Nellie. These two children became friends.

The years went by and Willy, now the young man, became known as Bill. His long distance relationship with Nellie had grown through letters. He looked forward to trips back to Lancaster to see her.

Nellie eagerly waited every day for the mail to arrive. She would take Bill's letters to a place of solitude to read them. She was falling in love.

Bill's Aunt Bertha described her in this fashion. "Nellie came to Sunday school carrying a little bouquet of dandelions grasped tightly in her little hand. She proudly gave them to her

Nellie Edith Osborne

teacher, who made a great show of being so pleased that Nellie thought of her. There never was a sweeter child or grown woman than Nell."

Bill and Nellie Edith Osborne married in 1916. They made their home in Eau Gallie, Florida. Nellie's mother, Edith, her stepfather Frank Morris and her brother Harold eventually moved to Miami. Bill and Nellie would often travel to visit them.

Nellie gave Bill a son, Phillip Osborne Roesch, born September 17, 1917, delivered by Dr. William Jackson Creel. His nurse was Beulah Houston. A baby shower was given with all family members in attendance. Pictures were taken to mark the special event, along with a list of gifts and whom they were from.

In 1918 Bill, Nellie and their one-year-old son Phillip moved to 25th Street North in Miami. Bill obtained a job as a bookkeeper for a real estate office. It was around 1922 that Bill's father enticed him to return to Eau Gallie to assume the position of editor at the newspaper.

Dr. Creel was the first resident physician to stay longer than two years, arriving in Eau Gallie in 1910. He lived on Highland Avenue with his wife, two sons and daughters. He would arrive at his patients' homes in any way that he could. Sometimes he would arrive by horse and buggy and other times by bicycle. (Source: Laura Houston Braddock)

In one summer he delivered 35 babies for a total of $38. Bartering became common practice during the depression. The good doctor would accept eggs, pies, lawn work and other items offered as payment for his services. He practiced medicine for 54 years. Everyone respected and trusted Dr. Creel. He was referred to as one of God's chosen people and the town named the new causeway spanning the Indian River for him.

Death Angel

The sorrow of losing a loved one is difficult and painful. The suffering can be unspeakable. But, when death strikes twice, a mother, and then a wife, within two weeks of one another, grief is like none other. Kind words from well-meaning friends and neighbors never seem to find anything remotely consoling; no matter how much they try.

Melbourne Times

September 10, 1924
BREVARD COUNTY'S LOSS

Mrs. (Ada Louise Houston) William R. Roesch, of Eau Gallie died yesterday at her home at the age of sixty-seven. She was born in 1857 at Enterprise, Florida and came to Eau Gallie in 1861 with her father John Houston widely known as the founder of this town. She was married in 1885 to William R. Roesch. The deceased is survived by her husband, a daughter Eva L. Roesch, a son, William Phillip Roesch, three sisters, Mrs. C. J. Young, of Ft. Pierce, Mrs. E. C. Sears, of Little River, Mrs. B. M. Stewart, Eau Gallie, and a brother C. M. Houston of Jacksonville.

Funeral services will be held today from the Eau Gallie Methodist Church at three p.m.

Her passing will be mourned by her family and a wide circle of friends.

Nellie became ill and family, friends and neighbors all expected she would most certainly recover. However, her condition continued to deteriorate. Bill rushed his wife to the Jackson Memorial Hospital in Miami where she would receive the best treatment available at that time. Here she would undergo surgery in an unsuccessful attempt to save her life.

Nellie Osborne Roesch,
In back yard of Old Oak Street home in Eau Gallie, Florida

Star Advocate, Titusville

September 26 1924
DEATH OF MRS. WILLIAM P. ROESCH

Wednesday morning the wires flashed the news back to Brevard County from Miami that Mrs. Nellie Osborne Roesch, wife of editor W. P. Roesch of Eau Gallie had passed away in Miami where she had been taken and where an operation had been performed in an effort to save her life. Mrs. Roesch had been rushed to the Jackson Memorial Hospital in Miami and everything known to surgical and medical skill was done in an unavailing effort to ward off the Death Angel. The news was a great shock to many of the friends of the family, which is one of the oldest in the county. Only a few close neighbors and relatives knew that she was ill and even these did not anticipate the tragic end. The sympathy of the entire county goes out to the grief stricken family. Only a short time before editor Roesch

*was called upon to give up his mother, a much-loved woman
of the Eau Gallie section. Tender hands performed the last sad
rites when Mrs. Roesch was laid to rest Wednesday afternoon,
and these same tender hands steeped in sympathy will follow
the bereaved husband and motherless little boy who are left
behind.*

It was difficult being a single father raising his young son, especially in the
early days of not only mourning his wife's death, but grieving over the loss of
his mother as well. He could barely care for himself and get to work.

Bill's half sister Lena was a Godsend helping her brother by caring for
her young nephew in any way she could. She loved them both. But, keeping
busy also helped Lena cope with the loss of her mother and sister-in-law.
On occasion she would take seven-year-old Phillip to Miami to visit his
grandparents, aunts and uncles. It was a welcomed diversion.

Sometimes Phil's Uncle Harold would come up from Miami and spend
a week visiting, giving Lena a break. While here he would sometimes take
young Phil to visit and place flowers on Nellie's gravesite. (Source: *Eau Gallie
Record*)

When Bill had to be out of town to attend business functions such as the
annual meeting of the South Florida Press Association in Tarpon Springs it
was especially helpful to have Lena caring for Phil. Being out of town at times
gave Bill an emotional break from the loneliness, sadness and emptiness he
felt at home without Nellie.

There were times he became frightened of losing his son.

Eau Gallie Record

December 25, 1925

*Phil Roesch, eight-year-old son of editor W. P. Roesch, has
been seriously ill with pneumonia. He is much better and his
physician expects him to be on the go again within a few days.*

Four Generations of Roesch Men (circa 1923)
Sitting: Philip, great-grandson Phillip Osborne and son William Russell
Standing: grandson William Phillip

The above photograph appeared in the *Herald Telephone* newspaper, the caption read, "This interesting group of fathers and grandfathers was photographed at Eau Gallie where they lived and enjoyed Florida Sunshine. They are Philip Roesch, 81 years old retired farmer and stockman of Lancaster, Wisconsin, and Eau Gallie; W. R. Roesch 58 years, fruit grower and resident of Eau Gallie and Indian River section for the past 40 years; W. P. Roesch, 32 years, editor-manager of the Eau Gallie Record and is a native of Eau Gallie, and Phil O. Roesch, now in training to assist his father in the Record office".

It was not initially Bill's intent to sell the *Eau Gallie Record*. He was after all training his young son Phil to take over the family business one day, just as his father had directed him from the time he was barely a teenager.

But, the hearts of both father and son were broken. Their daily lives were fractured by the deaths of Ada and Nellie and their spirits ceased to exist without them. Together, William and Bill made the difficult decision to sell the *Record*.

December 17, 1925
The Record Has Been Sold
The Eau Gallie Record has been sold. Edward Taylor, editor and publisher of the Melbourne Times, together with associates, are the new owners and under terms of sale will take charge of the

Record tomorrow, December 18th. We thank the people of Eau Gallie and Brevard County for the support and encouragement given us and bespeak of the new owners as a continuance of that famous Eau Gallie brand of cooperation, which has done so much to make the Record what it is today.
W.P. Roesch

William Phillip Roesch held the mortgage lien, Book 31, page 384.
One of the last entries the Roesch family made in the *Eau Gallie Record* was a message from the Mayor.

December 31, 1925
Mayor Roesch's Message
For 1926
May the peace and plenty of God rest upon this community all through the coming year, is the heartfelt wish of
Wm R. Roesch
Mayor of Eau Gallie

Bill moved on and accepted a position as foreman at the *Sentinel*. Newspaper accounts tell us, "He is a printer of many years experience in all branches of the business and to expect many improvements in the making of this paper and some classy specimens of the typographers' art from the presses of this plant." Here he is able to show his wit, with a few classic comments that could ring true today, in his own column titled:

Observations, By An Observing Observer
"An ordinary toad can flick its tongue out three inches and catch a fly, an ordinary woman can flick her tongue and spoil a reputation miles away."
"It takes a real strong man to lift a mortgage these days."
"A real cautious man can usually be identified as such at a glance - he wears suspenders and a belt and never takes chance."
"In view of the fact that gasoline and liquor won't mix without causing trouble this column suggests that the Eighteenth Amendment be enforced."
"In order to dress all a woman has to do is step-in slip-on and sing out "lets go".

"The ordinary flapper has a way of describing people and things that leaves very little to doubt her meaning - sidewalk loafers are called 'leg gazers' in the dialect of the day."

"Of all things that have changed during the past ten years, the 'parlor Joke' has gone the farthest".

...*Years Later*

Phil grew into a young adult and was good friends with Dr. Creel's son, William, known as Buzz. Their personalities were very similar and they enjoyed doing much of the same things, especially when it came to tinkering. Boys will be boys and they loved dismantling just about anything and then figuring out how to put them back together again. It was especially invigorating when they got it right and it worked.

So it wasn't entirely surprising when the day came that they started a radio and appliance repair business. Phil's grandfather, the Judge, gave the young men permission to set up shop on his property on Highland Avenue. Most jobs were to fix small appliances such as radios and toasters. Phil discovered he had a natural curiosity of how things operated and a talent for troubleshooting, but he was particularly intrigued with radios.

Larger appliances always called for a trip to the customers' home. One day such a request was received and they went out on a service call to repair a refrigerator. The methyl chloride somehow escaped and sprayed into the eyes of Buzz. Horrified, Phil rushed him to his father's medical office. Every conceivable treatment was exhausted, but this unfortunate accident left Buzz blind. Phil struggled to come to terms with what happened to his best friend, but he was inconsolable. He grieved over this incident the rest of his life. (Source: Elsie Louise Roesch Smith and Clyde Wilson Roesch)

Billy Dear

Florence Eloise Helen Sterling was the only child of Emond Lewis Sterling and Elsie Lovina Eldridge. Florence was born in Hattiesburg, Mississippi on July 3, 1904. She grew to be 5'4" with Hazel eyes, brown hair and a fair complexion.

The family came from Olean, New York, Elsie's hometown, and they were taking a trip to California. This was not just an ordinary vacation.

Florence and Jack were very much in love. He called her Billy. They eloped on January 18, 1923. Her parents made the announcement in the *Olean Evening Herald*, Olean, New York on February 1, 1923. It read:

Greene-Sterling

Mr. and Mrs. E. L. Sterling of 126 South Tenth Street announce the marriage of their daughter, Miss Florence Eloise Sterling to J. J. Greene, Jr., son of Mr. and Mrs. J. J. Greene, Sr. of Montpelier, Vt. that took place January 18th.

Mr. and Mrs. Greene left this afternoon on an extended wedding trip to include, New York, Boston and Rochester.

Her parents initially gave the appearance of being happy about the union, but something changed. Rumor has it that Florence became ill and her parents felt that her husband Jack was not caring for their only child properly and that she would be better off with them. Emond and Elsie drove from Olean, New York to Boston, Massachusetts where the couple was living.

It was raining as they drove Florence away from Jack as he stood on the sidewalk. She peered through the car rear window and cried out, "I'll be back Jack, I'll be back soon".

Jack tried to contact Florence to no avail. He wrote many beautiful love letters to her that her parents intercepted. She didn't see these until years later.

The following letter is dated March 8, 1923 mailed from the Back Bay section of Boston, Massachusetts where he and Billy were living after their marriage. Jack had no idea at this point in time that he would never see his wife again. He wrote:

"Dearest Wife,

"Billy dear, now that you are gone I realize how much I really love you. Dear girl, I'll never forgive myself for letting you go. Dearest, this room doesn't seem the same. I used to think it was so cozy and cheerful but now it seems so cold and bleak and dreary. Our kitchenette room is too full of memories of you. I see you at the gas range. I imagine I see you by the dresser curling your hair. The only thing that consoles me is the realization that you will return to me. And when you do, God knows how I'll stand it until then, you can gamble your last dollar that you won't leave me again.

"Dearest, I want you to rest and enjoy yourself while you are there. I won't ask if you had a safe journey, as God couldn't be so cruel as to make it otherwise.

"Well, dearest one, will close now hoping that you miss me as I do you. A wealth of love and a fortune of kisses from,

Your lonely husband, Jack."

Emond and Elsie Sterling were traveling via the Atlantic coastline sightseeing along the way to keep their daughter Florence far and away from Jack. When they reached the state of Florida, they heard about the land rush going on and decided to settle there.

Emond purchased a house in Eau Gallie on Pineapple Avenue. Just two blocks north of their home, he purchased land and then bought more land along the Indian River. The family settled into their new home and attended the Baptist Church on Highland Avenue. Emond, an entrepreneur, built the Rocky Water Tourist Camp on Pineapple Avenue. The shady campsites were offered for 25 cents a night or $1 a week. Emond also built 40

Emond Lewis Sterling and his wife
Elsie Lovina Eldridge

small cottages for guests to stay in for $1 a night and offered free shower baths, running water, a laundry room and firewood. He boasted that the grounds were located half way between "Jax-Miami", where you could enjoy fishing and boating on a beautiful spot on the Indian River.

The facility had a general store on the premises for their customers' convenience. On the shelves and in the coolers were bread, milk, a variety of cold drinks and all the necessary staples they may need for a picnic, a day at the beach or fishing. It was in here that his wife Elsie, who was always very much the lady, firmly placed a glass jar upon the counter. Whenever her husband uttered what she perceived as a distasteful word he was ordered to place a nickel inside that jar. Emond, who was not known to ever swear, always welcomed a challenge, and for his amusement, would from time-to-time retrieve a nickel from his pants pocket, and holding it tightly between his fingers would snap the coin into the jar, pinging it against the glass just to

Rocky Water Park

tease his wife. Good, bad or indifferent as the case may be, it saved enough money to pay for their road trip when they drove back home to visit family in Olean, New York.

The following ended the marriage of Florence and Jack.

"Judgment by W. H. Eldredge, Clerk of said State of New York, County of Cattaraugus." The annulment papers dated January 4, 1924 before the Honorable Charles H. Brown, reads as follows:

"Now on motion of John H. Ryan, counsel for the plaintiff, it is ordered, and judged and degreed, that the marriage between the said plaintiff, Florence Greenblat, and the defendant, Joseph Greenblat, also known as Jack Greene, be and the same hereby is dissolved and annulled, by reason of the consent of the said plaintiff Florence Greenblat having been obtained by fraud on the part of the defendant, and the parties are and each of them is freed from the obligations thereof. This Judgment is interlocutory but shall and become the final judgment here, granting the relief decreed three months after the filing and entry of this decision and judgment as of course, unless the court shall in the meantime for sufficient cause otherwise order. W. H. Eldredge, clerk of said county, and of the courts thereof, do hereby certify that I have compared the foregoing copy of Judgment with the original filed and entered in this office Jan. 7, 1924 and now remaining herein, and that said copy is a true transcript there from and of the whole of said original. In testimony whereof, I have hereunto subscribed my name and affixed the seal of said county, at Little Valley, this 7th day of January 1924."

(Jack never appeared at court. Was Jack really served papers to appear? W. H. Eldredge was a relative of Florence's mother. After all, Eldredge was her mother's maiden name. The true story of why this happened we will never know.)

Emond sold the campgrounds on July 9, 1925. The following appeared in the *Eau Gallie Record*:

ROCKY WATER TOURIST
CAMP SOLD
Popular Camp Located Just North
Of City on Dixie Highway Now
Under Management of
R. E. Perry

The Rocky Water Tourist Camp located on the Dixie Highway about one mile north of the city was sold last week by E. L. Sterling to R. E. Perry who is now in charge and will continue to operate the camp along the same lines followed heretofore.

Mr. Sterling and family left the latter part of the week for Olean, N. Y. where they will spend the summer months returning here in the early fall.

It is rumored that Mr. Perry has sold an option on the property to B. A. Stout of New York state, who will probably complete his purchase and obtain control of the camp by September first. However, the report could not be verified.

(I can tell you now the rumor was true.)

Marriage, Music and Moonshine

"This is to Certify that William P. Roesch of Eau Gallie in the State of Florida and Florence E. Sterling of Eau Gallie in the State of Florida were by me joined together in Holy Matrimony on the 31st day of July in the year of our Lord 1926." (Source: Marriage certificate.)

The newlyweds moved into the house on Old Oak Street that the Judge built. It sat just behind his home on Highland Avenue. It wasn't long before her nine-year-old stepson, Phillip, was calling her mom. Bill and Florence had their first child together 14 months later, a daughter, born October 15, 1927. She was named Elsie Louise after both of her grandmothers, Elsie Lovina Sterling and Ada Louise Roesch. Everyone called her Tiny. Two years later, 1929, the Great Depression began and life got more difficult with each passing year.

Elsie recalled the time when she was home sick with the whooping cough. "Dad was rarely home because he was always, at least seemed to be, working. If he did get home early, he would go fishing. This particular day I heard my father and mother talking just outside our living room door. I was only two years old at the time but clearly remember the event. I pulled my little chair over to the window and climbed upon it so I could peek out at my father as he was grabbing his net to go mullet fishing. I had watched him many times as he weaved or repaired his fishing nets. I slipped and fell off my chair breaking my left arm. To this day I still can't bend my arm up all the way.

"Our home was small and had only one bedroom, so my bed was in with my parents'. My Aunt Lena was living with us at this point in time. I remember her lovingly rubbing my back until I fell asleep. Later, she would slip out the back door and go to my grandfather's vacant house next door to sleep. In the morning she'd return." A porch off the kitchen had been enclosed for my brother Phil to sleep in.

By 1932 many banks had closed their doors. Money was difficult to come by, so Bill planted a watermelon crop hoping to bring in more cash. But that year there was a drought, and no rain fell on the field and the watermelon crop went to dust. Florence's mother bitterly complained to Bill that he was not providing, as he should be, for his family as she brought in bags of groceries. She had watched her daughter wilt to 97 pounds. But, Bill too had become a stick of a man. Frustrated, Bill wrote a letter on December 10, 1932 to the Honorable Noah Butt to apply for the postmaster position.

"Dear Colonel:

"In spite of the fact that for the first time in many long, lean years we of the Democratic faith are about to be allowed to come within smelling distance of the trough containing the dainty morsels known to the vulgar as federal jobs. Along with about sixty per cent of our citizens I am getting ready to make a play for the postmastership at Eau Gallie, and am taking the liberty of using your name as a reference as to my political faith, general cussedness and disability.

"Of course this is looking far into the future and anticipating what will happen, but when the time gets ripe I will certainly appreciate your support of my application.

"I believe I spoke to you one time about a slight change we want made in Eau Gallie's charter at the 1933 session of legislature, but being so full of political warring at the time I have forgotten the conversation. At present our City Clerk is an elective office and a number of us believe that it should be made appointive. Will it be necessary to advertise our intentions and if so how and for how long a time?

"Thanking you for past favors and awaiting your reply concerning above, I am,

Very truly yours,
W. Phil Roesch"

Noah Butt replied on December 13, 1932.

"I have yours of the 10th, and wish to advise you that it will be my pleasure to assist you, along the lines mentioned in your letter, at the proper time.

"When the time is right for such a move prepare for my signature such endorsement as you wish me to sign."

Two years later, on January 21, 1934 Bill wrote Noah Butt once again.

"Dear Colonel:

"Referring to our correspondence of December 1932 concerning my application for the postmaster's job in Eau Gallie.

"The Civil Service Commission will hold an examination about February 5th to fill this position. Should I be in the list of eligibles I will need your help.

"In the meantime I may have to call on you to help block a party who opposed your candidacy and who is now aspiring to help name one of his followers to the position.

"See you were able to have our friend Froscher's indictment thrown out—that was good work and I believe the case is closed now—hope so anyway.

"P.S. I have not forgotten the fact that I am indebted to you to the tune of a few dollars but, colonel, have you ever been broke? However, if the Lord or Mark Wilcox will smile on me maybe I can catch up again."

During these desperate times, Bill was pulling every political string possible. He had also written to E. A. Schurman, chief traffic inspector of the State Road Department applying for a job. The response was, "No vacancy has occurred wherein your services can be used."

Later that year, Bill received a copy of letter from Noah Butt that he had written to the Honorable J. Mark Wilcox, M.C. It read

"The undersigned, being a qualified Democratic elector and a patron of Eau Gallie, Florida post office, respectfully recommend W. Phil Roesch to you as my choice of those eligible for the position of Postmaster of Eau Gallie, and assure you any effort you may make toward securing such appointment for Mr. Roesch will be appreciated."

Ultimately, William was not appointed for the postmaster position. A year later, Florence began her food shopping at Kerrick's grocery store where they had a running tab. Once a week, Bill would go in and pay the bill. Eau Gallie was a safe community and Elsie Louise remembers walking to school and running errands all alone at the age of six and seven. There was only one street for her to cross, but with only a very few vehicles in town there was no need for concern. Her mother sent her to the store one day to buy half a dozen eggs. The eggs didn't come in cartons at that time, so they were placed one by one into a small brown paper bag and the cost added to their tab.

Along one stretch of the sidewalk there was a white picket fence.

Elsie, skipping along, placed the bag along the pickets of the fence and it bounced along home with her. The eggs were most assuredly broken and her mother never did complain, but she quickly salvaged what eggs she could by immediately putting them to good use. There was nothing you could afford to waste.

Elsie was a little over seven years old when her brother, Russell Sterling Roesch, was born on January 16, 1935.

Bill eventually quit his part-time job at the *Sentinel* and became a county police officer. He drove a motorcycle and would give Elsie rides in the sidecar.

Bill gives his daughter, Elsie, a ride

During prohibition, there was little enforcement of an unpopular federal law to shut down moonshine operations. But, as soon as a tax was to be collected on whisky, enforcement became more profitable for the local governments. Bill became a sheriff's deputy and in that capacity he closed down a few moonshine operations.

William Phillip Roesch Shutting Down Moonshine Operation

Florence played the piano and had accumulated a rather extensive collection of sheet music over the years. Phil played the trumpet and a friend of Phil's played the drums, so Florence joined them and the trio formed a band. They played Saturday nights at the Palms, a restaurant and lounge that overlooked the Indian River in Eau Gallie, as patrons danced to the music.

A Farm On Aurora Road

William Russell Roesch built a new farmhouse, around 1908, five miles west of his Highland Avenue home. According to his niece, Sue Stewart Seawright, William named the street leading to his home Aurora Road.

The name came from Aurora, Illinois, "The City of Lights". It was one of the first cities in the United States to implement an all-electric street lighting system in 1881 and it made quite the impression on the Judge when he saw it for the first time.

"My grandfather's modest three bedroom home was painted white with a porch across the front. It had a white picket fence with a gate that opened and shut with a latch. The back and sides of the yard had wire fencing. Once inside the gate, a dirt driveway led directly to a one-car garage.

" A variety of beautiful flowers were scattered about the property. But, the most beautiful were the many brilliant red geraniums that grew around the base of the house. A gourd was used to scoop out water from the well to water all the plants. Inside the home there were gas lamps that sat on tables throughout that burned a bright pure white light illuminating the home. A large brown bear rug with a huge head lay on the living room floor. The modest kitchen held a table, stove and icebox.

"When you walked out the side kitchen door, a foot path led around to the garage that sat to the back right side of the house. A very full chinese cherry tree grew on the left corner of the garage.

"Behind the house and behind the garage lay the land for farming. My grandfather had chickens and two cows. He grew squash, cucumbers, green beens, tomatoes, peanuts and watermelon. There were citrus trees of oranges, tangerines and grapefruit.

"Every year he would set up a long table on the right side yard and load it up with freshly picked watermelon for family, friends and neighbors to enjoy a big juicy feast. I loved the festive gathering.

"My grandfather taught me how to milk a cow and I was proud that I could. There were little foot bridges that went over the irrigation ditches; just the right size for me, a little girl of eight to cross." (Source: Memoirs of Elsie Louise Roesch Smith)

William was one of a very few people at the time to own a vehicle, a wooden platform truck, that he always parked inside the garage.

The roads were dusty dry sand and hub deep. High clearance vehicles were needed on account of the grass ridge in the middle. The roads were impassable for most vehicles. Oil pans and axeles were destroyed on the Model T. It wasn't until 1914 that a contract from the Brevard County Commission was issued to spread shell or rock over highways.

Highland Avenue and Aurora Road

The Judge married a widow, Elizabeth Meakin Carpenter Gwynne Roesch, a trained nurse, sometime between 1926 and 1929. Elizabeth was born on November 5, 1864 in British Columbia, Canada. She was always impecably dressed, whether she was going out or staying in, whether she expected company or not. She loved to entertain as often as she could, it could be friends or organizations, it really didn't matter. Her guests included the American Legion Auxillary that she would delight with an afternoon tea, and of course the ladies from the Eau Gallie Women's Club.

Promptly at 12 noon Elizabeth, better known as Lizzie, would ring the bell that was attached to the house just outside the kitchen door signaling the Judge that it was time to come in from the field for lunch. She also called him Judge. If there just happened to be a few friends in the house at the time, it was their hint to leave. (Source: Ora Lee Seawright Palmer)

No Place Like Eau Gallie

The community of Eau Gallie sits on the East Coast, just mid-way between Jacksonville and Miami. The Indian River, a two-and-a-half mile wide body of sparkling salt water, is separated from the Atlantic Ocean by a narrow strip of land. The area is noted for its near perfect climate conditions. Here flourish the orange, grapefruit and all other tropical fruits, grown to perfection.

Judge William R. Roesch penned, under the title "What Nature Has Done":

"With a lavish hand nature has bestowed upon this little city many things that have been withheld from other less favored localities.

"The best harbor for boats upon the entire East Coast of Florida. The Eau Gallie River where it joins the Indian River forms a large land-locked deep-water harbor, where many yachtsmen spend the winter season with their yachts, and have built a number of handsome winter homes upon its shores. Nature has been bountiful in the production of beautiful shade trees, so much appreciated in every climate, but doubly so in a land of perpetual sunshine."

Under the heading "What Man Has Done", Roesch extolled the existence of "several miles of hard surface streets, cement sidewalks, electric lights in homes and on the streets...good schools, churches and hospitable people."

"No place," penned Roesch, "has a brighter prospect for the future." He envisioned that the area would be "a populous center ranking with the first cities of the coast."

Eau Gallie was a close-knit community. Women of social prominence had their own association, the Eau Gallie Women's Club. The purpose was for "The Betterment of Our Town" and their motto was, "Not For Ourselves Alone". The club founded its first library for the town of Eau Gallie.

Programs consisted of, but were not limited to, a "Child Welfare Tea", "Americanism", "Sculpture", "Japanese Art" and "Crime Prevention". The meetings were held the second Tuesday of each month promptly at 3:00 in the afternoon in the home of whoever was hostess.

Florence Roesch was named press chairman of the club, a natural choice whereas her husband was in the newspaper business, and Mrs. William R. Roesch (Lizzie) was president. Some of the other members included Miss Lena Roesch, Mrs. W.H.H. Gleason (Flora), Mrs. William J. Creel (Jessie), Mrs. C.C. Houston, Mrs. Samuel K. Watts (Maud), Mrs. James W. Rossetter (Ella), Miss Ella F. Rossetter, Mrs. Ernest.B. Taylor (Mary), Miss Florence Hodgson, Mrs. James A. Seawright (Susan), Mrs. Jessie Stewart and Mrs. Ralph Stewart. Ada and Nellie Roesch were listed in memoriam.

Susan M. Stewart Seawright, was the daughter of Ada's sister, Isabel Margaret Houston Stewart, known as Belle. Susan was lovingly called Aunt Sue by just about everyone who knew her. She founded the Eau Gallie Women's Club, and was a lifetime member. She served as a board member of St. Paul's Methodist Church, member of Democratic Women's Club of South Brevard and the Harbour City Garden Club. She was a schoolteacher, member of the Order of Eastern Star and attended meetings with Lena. She was a life member of the PTA, belonged to the American Legion Auxiliary and the Eau Gallie Club. She was also a member of the Volunteer Firemen's Auxiliary and actively involved in many other organizations.

Homes For Sale

John Aspinwall of Barrytown, New York came to Eau Gallie with his wife Juliet to spend their winters. He purchased large parcels of land, and built his home on the south bank of the Eau Gallie River in 1890 and cultivated orange groves. They belonged to the St. John's Church and were among the first 29 communicants. Aspinwall also worked with Henry Flagler, the railroad magnate, to obtain the right of way for the railroad.

The Aspinwall family spent many winters here, until late December 1894 and early February 1895, when there was a terrible freeze and the Aspinwalls lost 150,000 pineapples and 800 orange trees. Devastated, he didn't return for another 10 years. The Aspinwall home was put up for sale. John was a great uncle to Franklin D. Roosevelt. The 32nd President of the United States named his sixth and last child John Aspinwall Roosevelt after his great uncle.

William also lost his groves and in the face of adversity worked to restore his fruit trees.

The House That Rossetter Built

James Wadsworth Rossetter came to Eau Gallie in 1902. He became known as a leader in the local fishing industry; he founded his own wholesale fishing enterprise. He became an agent for the Standard Oil Company.

The Rossetter house began with the purchase of the Houston slave quarters that William R. Roesch had expanded for his bride in 1885. Its front door faced Houston Street and the back door looked out to Highland Avenue.

Houston slave quarters facing Houston Street,
First home of William and Ada (Photo 2009)

To expand this house yet again, Rossetter purchased the Aspinwall winter home in 1908. It was taken down piece-by-piece then reassembled and connected to the expanded slaves quarters and first Roesch home with an open breezeway in between. Now its front door faced Highland Avenue, across the street from the Roesch House.

Side view of Rossetter House shows connection to addition.
It sits across the street from the Roesch House (Photo 2009)

Eau Gallie Record
Written by W.R. Roesch
Thursday, November 24, 1921
James W. Rossetter
Passed Away Sat'dy

On Saturday morning, November 19, at about one o'clock, death came to claim another one of Eau Gallie's prominent and respected citizens…identified with the upbuilding and development of this city for the past twenty years. He was born in Madison County in this state and was at the time of his death fifty-nine years of age.

For the past two years his health and strength had been failing, yet death came unexpectedly at this time.

During his residence here he always took a lively interest in anything pertaining to the upbuilding of the community of which he had become a real active part.

His friends were numerous; a large personal acquaintance over the state of Florida will regret to learn of his demise.

Personal friends and business associates here join the bereaved family, which consists of his wife, two daughters and three sons, and lament the passing of one who was an indulgent husband, a loving father and a kind neighbor.

Interment was made in the Eau Gallie cemetery at 10 o'clock on Sunday morning, a large concourse of friends following the body to its last resting place.

The family home was left to the Rossetter sisters, Caroline and Ella. Ella owned and operated an insurance agency. Caroline, known as Carrie, decided that she wanted to take her father's place as an agent for the Standard Oil Company. She applied to the board, but it expected her to fail within the year. Not only was she the very first female agent, she also successfully held the job for 62 years.

On April 14, 1945 the Rossetter sisters purchased the Roesch House across the street, and used it for storage.

Reunions and Recollections

It was in 1921 when Philip and Helen left Potosi, Wisconsin and moved to Lancaster to be near their children as they aged. On July 16, 1927, it is noted that Philip sold to his children, Ida, Ella, Clyde and Bertha, land he owned for consideration of love and affection and the sum of $1. The family remained close by holding family reunions that coincided with Philip and Helen's wedding anniversaries. These celebrations were something to behold.

The first recorded event took place on their 60th wedding anniversary, September 7, 1925. Newspaper accounts told of how the "Grant County Pioneers" celebrated with 200 dinner guests, under the friendly shade of trees at tables on the lawn at their home.

It was noted, "Mr. and Mrs. Roesch were still happy and hearty despite the vicissitudes of life."

Philip wrote a history of his life since coming to this country, which was read to all at the gathering. He told of his years in the army and highlights of his service. Philip recalled how he took part in the Siege of Vicksburg and marched with Sherman to the sea, and was in Columbia, South Carolina the night it was burned.

Philip recalled, "A lot of historians say the Yanks burned Columbia. Well, I was there the night the city burned and I know something about it. When the

Helen and Philip Roesch
70th wedding anniversary,
wearing their Civil War metals

95

Confederates evacuated Columbia, they left a lot of cotton throughout the town and set it on fire. The Union troops, labored to extinguish the fire and thought they had it under control. But in the night a high wind came up fanning the smoldering flames. The bales exploded like huge firecrackers. The flaming cotton was carried in every direction and in spite of all we could do, it spread to neighboring buildings and thus ignited most of the beautiful city."

He concluded by saying, "So this is our 60th wedding anniversary. It rained the day we were married so one should dispel any significance in the omen that a rainy wedding day means bad luck."

Philip & Helen Roesch Wedding Anniversary
and Roesch-Cardey Family Reunion

The celebrations took place again for the 65th, and on the 71st. Their 72nd anniversary was quietly observed with a few dinner guests at the home of their daughter, Mrs. Bertha Gibson. Helen was 92 and in poor health, and Philip at 95 was in good health but had lost much of his hearing. Philip concluded the festivities by saying, "And this is our 72nd wedding anniversary. We thank you all for being with us on this day."

———

When Philip came to the United States with his parents in 1857, he assumed, because he was a minor, he had became a citizen through his father, Mathias, when he applied for naturalization papers. With Philip being so politically active the entire community thought he was a citizen. Philip ran for public office and was elected. He also voted in every election. The first person he ever voted for was Abraham Lincoln when he ran for president. Philip also thought that because he subsequently served as a Union soldier in the Civil

War that he surely was a citizen. Philip, learning that such was not the case, applied for citizenship at the age of 95.

The *Grant County Herald* reported:

> *"The day arrived October 11, 1937 with much anticipation of Philip Roesch, aged 95 and Civil War veteran of Lancaster becoming a citizen."*
>
> *"It was unusually impressive as the ceremonies were carried out in circuit court on a Monday afternoon with family present to witness the event," the newspaper further reported. "Judge Sherman E. Smalley, whose duty and privilege it was to confer citizenship, swore Philip in. Smalley's father was Philip's captain during the great conflict. Smalley reported that his father had always held Philip in high esteem and that he had always been a loyal citizen. The official swearing in completed, delegations of patriotic orders stepped forward and presented Philip with bouquets, and many pictures were taken.*
>
> *"Following the presentation, Philip and his wife Helen received guests at their home. They had just celebrated their 72nd wedding anniversary last September. Mrs. Roesch is a native of this country. She was unable to be present in court, but, with her husband, received guests in their home in the Third Ward following the ceremonies."*

A separate Page One article follows:

The Grant County Herald
Lancaster, Wisconsin
Wednesday, October 13, 1937

CIVIL WAR VETERAN NATURALIZED

A naturalization of more than usual interest was that of Philip Roesch of Lancaster aged 95 years. Mr. Roesch was born in Baden, Germany May 11, 1842. He came to America in 1857 and located in Potosi Township. He served with credit throughout the Civil war and honorably discharged at the close of hostilities. He was now accorded citizenship in the county he fought so long ago to defend.

In Mourning

Fourteen months after Philip became a citizen, Helen suffered a fatal heart attack.

Grant Country Herald
December 3, 1938
Buried Monday

Mrs. Helen Roesch, 93 years old died at her home on December 3, 1938 following an illness of several months duration. She was a lifelong resident of Grant County. Burial was in British Hollow Cemetery.

Surviving the death of this highly respected lady are her 96-year-old husband, five children, eight grandchildren, twenty-one great grandchildren and one great great grandchild.

Fifteen months later, Philip joined his wife in death.

Grant County Herald
March 18, 1940
Death Summons Philip Roesch, Civil War Veteran, On Monday

Military Rites Held on Wednesday for Aged Citizen. Death brought an end to the long and eventful life of Philip Roesch at his home in his city at 8 o'clock last Monday morning, March 18, 1940 at the age of 97 years and 10 months. Until two weeks ago, Roesch was in his usual good health and took his daily walks and enthusiastic interest in life. Funeral services were held at 2 o'clock Wednesday afternoon at the Bagle-Wheeden

Funeral Home and interment was made in the British Hollow Cemetery, with military honors accorded by the local American Legion Post.

Although Mr. Roesch served in the United States Army and voted at each election, and held various public offices, he was not a citizen of this country. He had always supposed that his father had taken out naturalization papers, but, upon learning that this formality had never been carried out, Mr. Roesch, made application for naturalization.

At the time of the Armistice, in 1918 his old army overcoat with a bullet through the sleeve, although Mr. Roesch escaped injury, was cut to pieces in Potosi and the scraps given away as souvenirs as part of the celebration.

Mr. Roesch affectionately known to thousands as "Phil" was interested in both local and world affairs until his final illness. He loved children and was in turn loved by them.

Surviving his death are two sons Clyde of Potosi and William of Eau Gallie, Florida. William will not be here for his father's funeral. He is in such poor health that he is confined to his bed. Also surviving him are three daughters Mrs. Ella Gelbach, Mrs. Ida Korber, and Mrs. Bertha Gibson all of Lancaster; also 8 grandchildren, 22 great-grand children and one great great grandchild.

Fourteen months later, Philip and Helen's son joined them in death.

Melbourne Times
Death Claims The Judge
Eau Gallie Pioneer
Funeral Services Take Place Today
For W. R. Roesch
Long Time Resident Had
Been Prominent In Eau Gallie

Friday, May 2, 1941

William Russell Roesch, 74, died Wednesday after a long illness. Born in Potosi, Wis., July 8, 1866, he came to Eau Gallie in 1882.

Serving, as pallbearers will be John Hart, Jessee Karrick, E. B. Taylor, James McLendon, Mr. Simmons and Lansing Gleason.

Mr. Roesch had been a resident of Florida for 57 years, coming to the state from Wisconsin. While living in Eau Gallie he was postmaster for a number of years, later started the newspaper which at that time was called the "Eau Gallie Record," retiring from the paper to become mayor.

He also served as justice of the peace, head of the first Sunday school and builder of the Methodist Church. He was engaged in the nursery business.

Surviving are his widow, Mrs. Elizabeth Roesch, one son, William P., stepdaughter Eva Lena Dean, Eau Gallie; three sisters, Mrs. Ida Korber, Mrs. Ella Gelbach, and Mrs. Bertha Gibson of Lancaster, Wis.; and one brother, Clyde of Potosi, Wis.; three grandchildren, Phil of Eau Gallie, and Elsie Louise and Russell of Bonaventure.

Funeral services will be held Friday afternoon at the Methodist church. Rev. W. Hauck of Melbourne will preach the service assisted by Rev. B. Barrett. Brownlie Funeral Home has charge of the services.

The Governor's Niece

In the fall of 1884, Lieutenant Governor William H. Gleason was erecting a sawmill on Elbow Creek with his brother-in-law, Mr. Chauncy Carpenter. Chauncy was married to Gleason's sister, Elizabeth Rosabella Gleason who was known as Rosabella. The Carpenters arrived in Eau Gallie, Florida with their son, George W., and his wife, the former Miss Elizabeth Meakin, known as Lizzie.

The family stayed for a period of three years and upon completion of the sawmill, they all returned to their home, then in Washington territory. It was during this period that Lizzie first became acquainted with the Judge, William R. Roesch. The family often returned to Eau Gallie for visits.

Whereas George W. Carpenter was a nephew of William H. Gleason, his wife Lizzie was his niece by marriage. They had two sons, Arthur Ruby Carpenter, who was called Ruby, and John Chauncy Carpenter, who was called Chauncy.

When Lizzie's husband George died, she married again to a Mr. F. Gwynne and lived in Lakeland, Florida. When she was widowed a second time Lizzie returned to Eau Gallie at some point where she reconnected and married the widower William Russell Roesch.

The Judge died on April 30, 1941. Six weeks later, Lizzie left the home on Aurora Road, kept any and all personal items, much to the chagrin of her stepson, William Phillip Roesch and moved back to Seattle, Washington to live with her son Chauncy and his wife.

Lizzie

Melbourne Times
June 12, 1941
Mrs. Wm. R. Roesch left Tuesday for Seattle, Washington to make her home with her son and wife, Mr. and Mrs. Chauncy Carpenter.

Poor Aunt Lena

Eva Lena Houston, was born May 19, 1876, sharing her mother's birthday. According to her death certificate, Lena was Ada's natural born child, father unknown. William Russell Roesch unofficially adopted Lena and her surname was changed to his.

Lena was active in church, attending Sunday school and then Bible classes. She belonged to the Epworth League, which today is called the MYF, Methodist Youth Fellowship. She also belonged to and was an active member of the Order of Eastern Star, and the Eau Gallie Woman's Club.

Lena obtained a job in 1908 working in a printing office in Hastings, located 20 miles southwest of St. Augustine. She occasionally traveled home, a two-hours ride by train, to visit family. In 1910, after being employed for almost two years, Lena moved back to Eau Gallie and began working as a private housekeeper.

On June 22, 1927 at the age of 51 Lena married for the very first and only time to a widower, Clarence Egbert Dean, a gentleman 66 years of age who was born in Courtland, Ontario, Canada. He lived and worked for the railroad in Kansas City as a wheel oiler and then as a pipe fitter for steam engines. He moved to Eau Gallie to work for the Flagler Railroad that had been extended along the east coast of the state. Flagler provided homes with a front porch that sat along the edge of the railroad tracks for their employees.

Lena's happiness was short lived when Clarence died a year later. Lena moved back home with her father and stepmother, Lizzie. Lizzie wasn't the most sociable person toward Lena. Could the problem possibly have been the old adage of two women in the kitchen, a territorial situation?

According to the 1930 federal census, Lena was listed as a housekeeper for a private home. She was, at this time, living with her brother Bill and his wife, Florence, nephew Phil and niece Elsie Louise on Old Oak Street in Eau

Gallie. Lena would always give Elsie a quarter when she received payment for her housekeeping services.

Lena's husband Clarence had given her a gift of a beautiful ring. In the center was an emerald, which was her birthstone, with six round opal stones encircling it. At the tip and centered between each opal was a seed pearl. Lena felt wearing the opals brought her bad luck. She was very sad and cried much of time. She gave the ring to her 14 year old niece, Elsie, whereas opals were her birthstone. Elsie loved the ring and wore it for the next 65 years before passing it on to her daughter. Whenever Elsie reminisced about her Aunt Lena she would cry saying, "Aunt Lena led a very sad life."

Lena's death certificate states that she was admitted into the Brevard County Farm in Titusville, Florida on May 6, 1942, apparently due to illness. While there she was under the care of a physician. Three months and six days later, Lena passed away on August 12, 1942 at the age of 67 years, 2 months and 24 days.

Eva Lena Houston Roesch Dean

Lena's obituaries:

Melbourne Times
Eau Gallie Resident
Died Wednesday

August 14, 1942

Funeral services were held Thursday afternoon in Eau Gallie for Mrs. Eva Lena Dean, 67, who died at her home in Eau Gallie Wednesday. The Rev. G. E. Bennett officiated.

Pallbearers were John Hart, Pat Stewart, Arthur Simmons, Bill Carter, K. O. Kerrick and H.I. Spiller. The Eastern Star had charge of the services at the grave.

Funeral arrangements were in charge of the Brownlie Funeral Home.

(Note: The family, desiring privacy, listed Lena as dying in her home in Eau Gallie.)

Titusville Star Advocate
Eau Gallie News
Florence E. Roesch, Correspondent
Funeral Thursday
Tuesday, Aug 18, 1942

Eau Gallie, Aug. 17—Funeral services were conducted Thursday for Mrs. Lena Dean at the Methodist Church, with Rev. G. E. Bennett in charge. The Eastern Star of Melbourne had charge of the services at the cemetery.

Mrs. Dean was the former Miss Lena Roesch, having been born here. She resided here all her life. Surviving are one brother William P. Roesch, two nephews Phillip and Russell, also one niece, Elsie Louise.

Florence loved her sister-in-law. It must have been difficult for her to write the foregoing obituary.

Alligators and the WPA

On September 29, 1931, Emond and Elsie Sterling began a new multi-faceted enterprise. They purchased a garage with a wooden canopy that hung over the gas pumps from Mrs. Emma M. Dealing, widow of Paul B. Dealing, on September 29, 1931 for the sum of $10. It included all automobile accessories, one Ford truck, all parts, equipment and tools.

This land was originally owned by the United States of America, and on June 10, 1884 pursuant to the Homesteads Act of May 1862, was sold to Joseph Brady Bower. It was signed and recorded by President Chester A. Arthur. Bower then sold a portion of the land to the Jacksonville, St. Augustine & Indian River Railway Co. for the sum of $1. (Source: Abstract Title)

Emond renamed it Sterling's Garage, an Amoco station, in Bonaventure, Florida about 12 miles north of Eau Gallie and five miles south of Cocoa. It sat between Dixie Highway (Route 1) and the Indian River.

Sterling Garage and Snack Stand

On December 15, 1944, a big Suddath moving van lost control and ran over three gas pumps and caused the canopy to collapse. The canopy was never rebuilt.

The house started out as an existing small two-bedroom home that sat on the hill behind the station. Emond moved it down the hill so it sat adjacent to the left side of the garage. He then proceeded to build an addition to create a rambling four-bedroom cottage style home painted white. He also built three cottages that he rented out to vacationers and later to military families. One cottage sat to the right of the garage, the other two sat on the hill connected by a carport.

The expansive kitchen on the main house, roughly 20 X 26, located in the front, was turned into a restaurant. Apparently, Elsie and Emond suspected that their daughter's marriage to Bill was in jeopardy. So, they built the lunchroom in preparation for her to manage as its chief cook and bottle washer. Now Florence would have the opportunity to earn an income and provide for her children. Shortly thereafter she filed divorce papers and moved home. Phillip, now 19 years old, stayed behind with his father.

Florence dug right in, helping her parents in all facets of the business. She also became a correspondent gathering and providing Eau Gallie news for the *Titusville Star Advocate*.

The room, with four-inch wide pineda pine floors and windows lining the walls on both the north and south sides, was bright and cheery. A narrow counter standing about five feet high separated the working kitchen from the dining area.

Just inside the front door entrance and to the right was a two-hinged blue partition that concealed a small white round porcelain sink where customers could wash their hands before sitting down to lunch at one of the cheerful tables. On the menu was a T-bone steak dinner, including salad, bread, drinks and dessert all for just 99 cents.

Out the side screened kitchen door that always slammed shut, and down two wooden steps, was the entrance into a small rustic stand. Families that rented the cottages and customers that stopped to refuel their vehicles would make their way over to the open window located under the front wooden awning to purchase honey, jellies, crackers, whoopee pies, canned goods, bread and non-filtered cigarettes that sold for 20 cents a pack or cigars. Hot thirsty travelers mostly purchased bottles of soda pop that were pulled cold and wet from the large red Coca Cola cooler. The children tended to favor either the grape or chocolate soda. In front of the stand, just beyond the awning, Emond built a wooden tiered shelf to display oranges, tangerines and grapefruit that he also sold.

Left to Right: Florence Eloise Helen Roesch, Elsie Lovina Sterling,
Emond Lewis Sterling holding Russell Sterling Roesch and his sister, Elsie Louise Roesch
Standing in front of lunchroom, fruit display and stand (circa 1936)

He advertised "Sterling's Service Station, Lunch Room and Cabins, Gas and Oil, and Famous Indian River Fruit".

Customers were amazed to find two sizable alligators on display. Emond had dug a pit large enough to hold the reptiles. He created a wading pool by cementing half the area and the rest was left sandy so they could sun themselves. To feed these carnivorous beasts, he would put a raw piece of meat, particularly chicken, on the end of a stick that slid between the thick iron fencing that caged these animals. For safety, it kept them in and people out. It was quite the show, all intended to entertain and keep customers returning.

Years later, he released them to the expansive swampy area across the Dixie Highway. But, they kept returning. It took a half a dozen tries before the alligators decided to accept their new abode.

Bill and Florence's divorce was finalized on June 18, 1936. It is believed by some that the loss of Bill's first wife Nellie was so utterly devestating to him, that he was unable to be the kind of husband he should have been to Florence, to whom he was married for almost 10 years. Perhaps he married again too quickly, perhaps looking for a mother for his son Phillip. But then again, Florence could have been on the rebound from her annuled marriage.

Florence met a widower, Virgil Scott Hilligoss, when he was hired by her father in 1934 to work as a mechanic at the Sterling Garage during the later part of the depression. Everyone called him Scott or Scotty. His love of cars evolved at the age of 20 when the Indy 500 car races began on Memorial Day, May 30, 1911. He was a big fan and never missed attending the event no matter where he was residing, ever.

Scott was born in Jefferson, Indiana, and at the age of 23 he married Klondia. The next two years blessed them two lovely little girls. Scott was 25 years old when his wife died leaving him with two babies. He moved to Detroit, Michigan and lived with his in-laws so they could help him raise his daughters. He went to work for a time at the Henderson Motorcycle Company.

Once his daughters were grown and married, Scott moved to Florida to provide a warmer climate for his 84-year-old mother's failing health. He rented the cottage next to the Sterling Garage and lived there until her death in 1937.

The Great Depression left many without work and means to support a family. A Presidential executive order was issued in 1935 to help the country get back on its feet. The Works Progress Administration program began to generate jobs for the unemployed. Later in 1939 the name was changed to Work Projects Administration, known as the WPA.

Scott was a strong, hard working man with a great sense of humor. His reputation as a good and honest mechanic traveled fast. But, whenever he saw the WPA coming down the highway he would remark, "Here comes the WPA, water, piss and air." Scott knew when they stopped at the station this would be all they would ask for, free service.

It became apparent after a time that Florence was quite attracted to Scott. It took a few years, but finally they began to date.

Love and War

In 1943, Florence performed her military duty by becoming a volunteer of the Aircraft Warning Service of the U.S. Army during World War II.

Elsie Louise recalled, "The entire family took their turns operating a 24-hour plane spotting station. These stations were placed in various locations throughout the state. When a plane was within sight, or hearing distance, we would call in to a central location and report the direction, speed, altitude and number of engines. That way, the government kept track of any unauthorized planes."

Phil was more like a son, rather than a stepson to Florence; after all, she raised him. He joined the Army and he would write her V-Mail letters, addressed to "Dear Mom". Sometimes he drew cartoons on his letters. The v-cartoon became highly popular and used very creatively by the servicemen.

Soldiers wrote their letters on a form the military provided. It was then photographed, placed on 16 mm motion picture film and transported in a mail sack that carried approximately 136,000 letters. The film was next enlarged to 4 X 5 wet prints that were dried and sliced into individual letters. There were a total of 19 military v-mail stations across the United States that provided this service. This saved storage space for the transport of other necessary items during the war.

Scott received a telephone call from a company he once worked for in Detroit. The facility was going to be building engines for military jeeps that would be shipped overseas upon completion to the soldiers. Scott was the best and most knowledgeable man they knew for the job. Wanting to make a contribution for the war effort, along with the enticement of great pay, he gladly accepted.

The separation made Scott realize just how much he had come to love Florence and her children, Elsie and Russell. Whenever possible he'd drive back to Florida to see her and the kids. Sometimes he would arrive in the middle of the night. When morning came Florence would find Scotty sleeping in his car. She would tap gently on the car window to wake him and soon he was in the kitchen eating a hardy breakfast. Then with a big grin he would tease Elsie about becoming a farmer's wife some day.

It was during WWII, that Bill Roesch decided the old newspaper press on which the *Eau Gallie Record* was started 35 years ago could be used in helping to win the war by turning it into ammunition.

Printing Press

He wrote a letter to the *Melbourne Times*, stating:

> *"Notice in your issue of August 7 where Melbourne has started a 'Junk Drive' to collect scrap metal for our war effort. I have on my Eau Gallie property, the frame of a Washington Hand Press, which, as you know, is of cast iron and weighs in the neighborhood of 500 pounds.*
>
> *"This press is the one used by my father in starting the Eau Gallie Record in 1907 and to the best of our knowledge had over a hundred years of service behind it at that time. If the Salvage Committee will accept this metal, I will be glad to donate it."*

Beneath the Mulberry Tree

Scott returned home when the war came to an end and resumed his duties as a mechanic at the Sterling Garage. He and Florence were taking a trip to Orlando and decided to go to Sanford instead where they married on April 8, 1944. They surprised the family with the news upon returning home.

Emond sold the Sterling Garage that was now a Gulf station to Florence and Scott on May 21, 1949. Emond and Elsie then retired to the cottage on the hill that sat to the right of the carport. Emond was known as Gramp and Elsie was known as Gram. In their front yard grew an orange tree and a beautiful, large, red hibiscus plant. Then there was this big old Mulberry tree. There were many great tasting pies made from the berries. Gramp would sit under the breezeway to keep out of the hot sun; carving beautiful walking canes out of orange tree limbs. Each handle would be uniquely designed with the head of a pig or an alligator, still others with curved shapes. He passed away in 1953 at the age of 84.

Gram could be found many days sitting in her screened-in porch. She loved to play Chinese checkers; no one could beat her as she told stories of when she and Gramp dated in the horse and buggy days. Her laugh was somewhat of a giggle. She enjoyed crocheting and was also a pretty good cook. Every morning she would braid her long hair and wrap them up and over her head. Her chestnut hair may have turned gray and her soft hands wrinkled with age, but she always remained young at heart.

She loved the birds and they loved her, too. She would go out on her front stoop to feed them. They would actually eat bread from the palm of her hand. The birds waited for her each and every day just outside her front-screened door. If she were late, the birds would fly around to the back where the porch was located and call out to her by chirping quite loudly. "Okay," she'd say, "I'm coming." The birds would then fly back around to the front of the cottage and wait for her to appear. The blue jays she called little pigs because they would chase away the little birds not willing to share at all. So she would shoo them away to make sure the red-winged blackbirds, cardinals, orioles and others got their fair share.

Gram at the age of 85 could still bend over and touch her toes without bending her knees. With her last breath, she stretched her arms outward as if reaching for someone and called out, "Emond". She died in 1961 at the age of 91. Gram and Gramp were cremated and laid to rest beneath the Mulberry tree. Eventually they would be moved and buried with their daughter Florence and her husband Scott.

Elsie Louise And Her Sailor

World War II was in full force on October 8, 1942 when nineteen-year-old Robert Franklin Smith enlisted in the Navy in Bridgewater, Massachusetts. He was stationed at the new Banana River Naval Air Station in Cocoa Beach, Florida that was located across the street from the Atlantic Ocean. In 1948 the base was transferred to the United States Air Force and then in August of 1950 it became known as Patrick Air Force Base.

Shortly after Bob's arrival, he met Elsie Louise Roesch at a local dance hall where her mother was one of the chaperones for the evening. With permission from her mother, the two began dating, fell in love and were married at the courthouse in Sanford, Florida by Judge Ware on April 22, 1943, six months after they met.

Their first home as husband and wife was the small cottage on the hill that sat to the left of the carport. A short time later they moved to the larger three-room cottage at the foot of the hill that sat to the right of the garage.

Their first child was born on September 7, 1944, a daughter they named Kathryn. While still in the hospital, a hurricane warning was issued. It was first detected on September 9, northeast of the Lesser Antilles. It likely developed from a tropical wave

*Elsie Louise Roesch and
Robert Franklin Smith*

several days before. It moved west northwestward, and steadily intensified to a 140 mph (230 km/h) major hurricane on the 12th, northeast of the Bahamas. The Miami Hurricane Warning Office designated this storm The Great Atlantic Hurricane, to emphasize its intensity and size, which appears to be the first time a name was designated by the office that evolved into the National Hurricane Center.

The cottage still stands today and has been repaired after sitting empty for many years minus the screened-in porch. (2009)

All patients at the Naval Base Hospital had to be evacuated. Elsie and her new baby girl were put into the back of a military jeep that drove them over a wood plank bridge that crossed the Indian and Banana Rivers to a school in Melbourne and given a cot to lie on. Elsie said, "I felt every bump going over that bridge." They were later moved to a very small Melbourne hospital after the men were moved out of one ward to make room. This hospital that turned into a motel, has now been torn down.

Unknown to Elsie and the hospital staff, her mother, Florence, had arrived at the base to take them home just as they were being driven away before the storm hit. Bob went into a panic trying to find his wife and daughter. It took him and Florence until the next morning to find them, partly because the military kept moving them about. Thankfully, the hurricane turned northward and on the 14th it hit the Outer Banks.

In February of 1945, the Navy sent Bob to Oak Harbor, Washington, accompanied by his wife and daughter. Then in six months they were off to Seaside, Oregon. Several months later, Elsie flew back to Florida when Bob was shipped off to National City, California, a suburb of San Diego. Two months later, she rejoined her husband in California. She followed her husband, when allowed, to each and every port with their daughter.

Bob's next port was China and Elsie was advised it would not be a safe place for her and their daughter to go to due to civil unrest. So Elsie returned home to Florida to wait.

Bob was on the U.S.S. LST-9 (Landing Ship, Tank) ship, which is an amphibious vessel designed to unload tanks, troops and supplies. They were enormously helpful in times of war and peace. While passing by Okinawa on its way to China, the Japanese who didn't know the war was over, fired upon the ship.

Then in January 1946, the ship pulled into port at the Whangpoo River in Shanghai, China, which flows into the Yangtze River. Bob was assigned to build stables on the American ship for Chiang Kai-shek so he could transport his horses. This was during the pre-communist era when the U.S. supported General Chiang against the Communist's People's Liberation Army led by Mao Zedong in the civil war for control of China. The commuist party did assume control after two decades of war and the People's Republic of China was establish on October 1, 1949.

Bob sadly recalled, "Baby girls in China during this period were not valued, and were thrown into the Yangtze River to drown. It was horrible seeing dead babies floating in the water." Bob called his wife and told her what was happening and that there was this baby girl he wanted to adopt. Elsie agreed and told him if that was what he wanted to do it was fine by her. But, the military wouldn't allow it.

Bob returned home and was stationed in Jacksonville, Florida where his wife and daughter joined him. Then in 1947, Bob was sent to England. In order to join her husband, Elsie boarded the U.S.S. Ernie Pyle out of New York with her daughter and sailed to Bremerhaven, Bremen, Germany, which is a port city situated along the Weser River. The journey required an overnight stay and while in their room they heard beautiful German music playing. They left their room on the second floor and quietly descended the staircase until they reached a point where they could overlook the banquet hall. Here they sat down upon a step and enjoyed the music.

The next morning they took a flight out of Bremanhaven to London, England and then a train to Plymouth, England where she met up with Bob. The area had four blocks of nothing but brick rubble left by bombs during WWII. But a path had been cleared that led to a theater. While stationed there, Elsie recalled that King George VI and Queen Elizabeth arrived to dedicate the rebuilding of Plymouth.

Bob was discharged in 1948 and he and his family moved to his hometown in Massachusetts. He obtained a job working nights at a leather mill and he joined the Reserves, bought land and built a starter two-room house. In the spring of 1951, Bob was called back to serve one final tour of active duty during the Korean War. This time, Elsie stayed home.

Over the years they were blessed with four daughters. Elsie worked in a commercial insurance office and was an active member in the community. She served on the town's finance board, joined a citizens group and taught Sunday school. Elsie was the only one of Bill's four children to leave Florida.

Fourth Time a Charm

Bill decided to move to Miami sometime after his divorce from Florence. He obtained a job with an awning company. He rented an apartment from a German woman whose name was Gertrude Maria King, and they soon were dating. They were married at the court house in Key West on April 7, 1940. This third marriage ended almost as soon as it began when Gertrude sought and was granted a divorce. Bill moved back to Eau Gallie.

Bill finally found true love again with Marjorie Emma Wilson, daughter of Louis Henry Wilson and Evelyn C. Braddock. They were married on July 19, 1943; she was 22 years young and Bill was 52. Their son, and Bill's fourth child, Clyde Wilson Roesch, was born February 23, 1945, named for his great Uncle Clyde in Wisconsin.

Bill's oldest son Phil was close to his dad, so he was around his little brother Clyde often. Since Florence had raised Phil, he grew up with and was close to Elsie and Russell as well. Marge wanted Clyde to know his siblings, Elsie and Russell, so she would bring him over to Florence's home for visits. The age difference was just too great and the relationship just didn't have the opportunity to develop.

Clyde Wilson told how years later, "My father went to the barn where he had stored a muzzel loading rifle still scarred with a chop mark on the barrel from a saber during a battle one of his grandfathers was in. The old rusty gun was in bad shape. The rifle originally was

Marjorie Emma Wilson Roesch

118

a flintlock but was later converted to a percussion cap. The old gun was even then in two pieces and totally non-functional; it likely sometime in the first half of the 1900s was stored in an open environment and may have been that way when dad got it. I would suppose that dad's dad or his Uncle Clyde gave him the gun. When I got my hands on the rifle dad just sort of turned it over to me with a brief on the history of the gun totally without any fanfare. I tried to clean the gun up a bit but the rust had brought ruin long before."

Sheriff William Phillip Roesch with sons Phil and Clyde

Bill never believed that there were many truly religious men of the cloth in the world; he really didn't trust them. From a window in his home he would watch this one particular man walk by every day carrying his bible. Bill never knew exactly where the man was going, but felt this man was truly a man of God. He decided that upon his death he wanted the Masons from his lodge to perform his services. This comes as no surprise, for Bill was a devoted and past Master of Melbourne Lodge 143, Free & Accepted Masons.

It takes seven years from the time of becoming Junior Steward, to progress up the line of succession to become the Master Mason, which is the highest ranking of all Lodge officers. As Master, his word is final over any and all actions pertaining to his Lodge. He is responsible for every lodge officer and their duties, every lodge committee, ritual, social function and fundraiser.

Bill and Marge were happily married until Bill's death February 8, 1960. On February 24, Marge wrote Bill's daughter a letter.

"Dear Elsie,

"Thanks so much for your call. Bill hadn't felt too well since his heart attack back in 1957. Then a week or ten days before he died he started feeling bad. About nine o'clock that night he started having a little trouble breathing then at ten o'clock he asked me to take him to the hospital.

"They kept Bill under oxygen all night and took him off next morning. It was cut down in the night. I wanted to stay all night again the next night, but Bill was so much better, that he insisted I go home so I could be back early next morning to take him home. He held my hand real tight just before I left and said, 'I'll be so glad to get home again'. At twelve-twenty (in the morning) the telephone rang. The doctor was calling. The doctor said that apparently he died in his sleep with no pain.

"Russell and his wife have been here quite a lot and have offered their help in every way. They have certainly been nice too. You have some very sweet brothers – including Clyde, of course. All three of them have a very sweet sister too. I get more proud all the time that I'm a Roesch, love, Marjorie".

MELBOURNE TIMES

Mr. W. P. (Bill) Roesch, 66, Palm Bay, died Monday at a local hospital. Mr. Roesch who was born in South Brevard, was a conservation agent for the State Board of Conservation covering South Brevard.

He was a past master of Melbourne Lodge 143, F&AM, and had served as peace officer in Brevard County since 1926.

Survivors are the widow, Marjorie W. Roesch, three sons, Phil O. Roesch and Clyde W. Roesch both of Palm Bay, and Russell S. Roesch, of Cocoa: a daughter, Mrs. Robert Smith, Bridgewater, Mass and nine grandchildren.

Funeral services will be at 2 p.m. Thursday at Brownlie Funeral Home with burial in Eau Gallie Cemetery. Masonic services will be held by the Melbourne Lodge.

NASA and Phillip

Phillip Osborne Roesch loved repairing radios as a young man with Buzz Creel and he always remained curious about how they worked. Being the intelligent man that he was, Phil built upon his experience, working in maintenance and repair of the electrical systems in the Oleander Hotel that sat on the corner of Pineapple Avenue and Eau Gallie Boulevard. The hotel was torn down some years ago and a restaurant took its place. He then worked for a time as electrician's helper for an electrical contractor before going back to being a radio repairman for the Huggins Supply Company.

After a stint in the U.S. Army, Phil returned home to Eau Gallie, Florida, and married Dorothy Carpenter who was originally from Tennessee. There is no known relationship to Elizabeth Carpenter. For a time they lived in the house on Old Oak Street, behind the Judge's house, where he as a child once lived with his parents, Bill and Nellie, and then later with Bill and Florence. At some point, Phil and Dorothy moved to Cocoa, Florida where he began his own radio and appliance service business. They had three children, two daughters and one son.

All his past experience prepared him for the most interesting and challenging

Left to Right: William Phillip with son Phillip Osborne and Phil's wife Dorothy Carpenter standing in front of Old Oak Street home in Eau Gallie

job of his lifetime. In 1951, at the age of 34, he obtained a position with RCA, a subcontractor for NASA, working at Patrick Air Force Base. In seeking out an explanation of what he did, Phillip replied as if it could be understood, "I calibrate the equipment used to calibrate the monitoring instruments that are used to record the missile telemetry and other in-flight information and support activities."

It was always a top secret when and what time military missiles were going to be launched. NASA (National Aeronautics and Space Administration) certainly didn't want the Russians knowing this information or anyone else that might have an interest. Phil couldn't even tell Dorothy. She would only know by waking up in the morning and finding him gone from their bed.

Philip Osborne Roesch, Electronics Specialists

Phil was involved with Cape Canaveral from the very early beginnings of space exploration. There were various times he would be sent "down range" to Antigua, West Indies; Grand Turk, Ascension and other islands to monitor missile activities in that corridor. Part of the monitoring was to pinpoint the recovery location of early pre-man missions of returning monkeys. The first to return home safely on May 28, 1959 were Able, a rhesus monkey, and Miss Baker, a squirrel monkey. These animals were launched to study the biological impact on man during space flight.

It was on May 5, 1961 the first manned Mercury spacecraft lifted off with Astronaut Alan B. Sheppard that lasted a total of 15 minutes. These missions took place during Phil's first 10 years of employment. Phil, as communication manager, ultimately supervised a staff of 19 technicians and radio operators, directly in maintenance and operation in a number of communication center facilities. (Source: Clyde Wilson Roesch and Elsie Louise Roesch Smith and Resume of Employment, Phil O. Roesch)

His brother Clyde said, "I remember Phil stewing over transistors and the new component chips. He was going through a transition from vacuum tube to transistor technology."

Phil and Dorothy's marriage ended in divorce after 20 years.

The last time Bill's children, Elsie, Russell and Clyde, were together was at the funeral of their brother Phil who died of lukemia August 2, 1988. There was no conversation between them this day.

Pastor Russell and Lucky Clyde

Russell graduated from Cocoa High School where he was involved in baseball and football. He went to work as a part-time news correspondent for the *Miami Herald* writing sports. He was so talented that the paper wanted him full-time. But that would mean moving to Miami and that was just out of the question for him, too far from family.

He married Ola Kathryn Watts, known as Kathy, in 1954, the daughter of an American Baptist Minister. They lived in the cottage on the hill on the left side of the carport. Eventually, they combined the two cottages into one home. They had five children, three sons and two daughters.

Pastor Russell Sterling Roesch and wife Ola Kathryn Watts

Russell became a mechanic at Wienberg-Schumaker Gulf Oil Station in downtown Cocoa. But the oil crises in the mid 1970's forced the business to close. It was while he was working at the garage that Russell believes he received his calling and in 1971 he was ordained and assigned as pastor to the American Baptist Church. He later reopened the Sterling Garage that had been closed since Scott's, his stepfather's, death.

Clyde joined the Army shortly after his 17th birthday. He was stationed first at Fort Gordon, Georgia. Next came assignments to Fort Monmouth, New Jersey; Fort Knox, Kentucky; and Fort Ord, California. For the last 20 months of his military service, he served in the Third Armored Division at Friedberg, Germany.

"It (Germany) was the one place where my name Roesch was pronounced correctly. My Army days I found frustrating and entertaining at the same time; it was a 'peace time' period of 'no shots fired'. For that I suppose I was a lucky Clyde. Vietnam was starting to fire-up about the time I was discharged." Clyde has a wonderful dry sense of humor.

Clyde Wilson Roesch and wife Nancy Caldwell Pomeroy
Wedding Day Feb. 20, 1971

After being discharged from the Army, Clyde lived in Punta Gorda on the west coast of Florida for about eight months working for Tri-County Engineering. Clyde decided to call a friend he went to school with in Melbourne, Florida. Distance didn't get in the way of true love and this friend, Nancy Caldwell Pomeroy, and he married on February 20, 1971.

They moved to Flagler County, Florida where Clyde went to work for ITT

Community Development in the engineering and land-surveying branch. They had two sons.

In 1970, Clyde was given the compass his grandfather, William R. Roesch, used in land surveying. It had been stored for years.

Rossetter Foundation

In November of 1992, the Rossetter sisters donated their home, known as the Rossetter House, and the Roesch House to the Florida Historical Society. The women established an endowment, The Rossetter Trust Fund of $2.85 million dollars, for the society to preserve and maintain not only the property, but their family history as well for a lifetime.

Today the Roesch House is headquarters for the Historic Rossetter House Museum and Gardens offices, welcome center and Ella's Closet gift shop. It displays items and photos of the Rossetter family. Tours are given of the Rossetter House that contain their personal belongings. The lovely grounds are rented to provide a beautiful backdrop for weddings.

In 1947 representatives of the Houston family deeded the historic Houston Cemetery to the Eau Gallie Garden Club with the understanding that the picturesque resting place of their ancestors, the first settlers of Eau Gallie, would be preserved and maintained. To continue its preservation, the Garden Club eventually turned the cemetery over to the Florida Historical Society. Today it is part of the Rossetter Museum complex and is supported by the Rossetter Trust Fund.

A chain-link fence with unlocked gates surrounded the cemetery. After it was vandalized and to protect the few gravestones that remained, the Rossetter Foundation installed a wrought iron fence.

Strictly for entertainment, patrons are asked to bring their cameras for a Ghost Tour of the facilities. Then there is the Old Eau Gallie Murder Mystery Tour to play the game of who done it inside the Rossetter House.

Time marches on; nothing stays the same. The Roesch family marched forward and somehow lost its history along the way. But it was just below the surface waiting to be rediscovered, waiting for their story to be told.

The Roesch family throughout history was very public and unique in that they left a trail of information through diaries, memoirs, news articles and photographs. They were loyal to each other and proud to be Americans. They served their country honorably through military service and contributed to society by working and volunteering to help create better communities.

They called out, find me, and a forgotten past is no longer.

Family Gathering

Everything must be perfect for this very special occasion that actually began two and half years ago, I thought, particularly for my mother, Elsie. I recalled the events that led to this day as I went about preparing a luncheon I hoped everyone would enjoy and tidying up the condo we had rented in Cape Canaveral, Florida.

When my father became ill, it became an urgent need to gather as much information as possible about my family history before another generation was lost, not *just* to me, but also to the generations yet to come. I had heard bits and pieces, but they formed a puzzle; nothing seemed to fit. What a wondrous adventure the last few years had been, uncovering so many details. How amazing it was to connect with a cousin I never knew I had, the son of my mother's half brother Clyde. Now we would all become acquainted because of that chance meeting on the Internet. "Who would have thought?" I mused.

It was the first day of spring in 2008 when Elsie's husband, Robert, quietly passed away in a Massachusetts nursing home with family surrounding him with love. "All but for me, " I sadly remembered with guilt. I had just talked to him by phone two days before. When I told him that I wanted him up and running around when I got back, I could picture him grinning his wide toothless grin, wearing his favorite red New England Patriot's football cap, as he replied in a stronger voice than usual, "Yes."

I remember that sorrowful day in March, being here with my husband in this very same Florida condo when the telephone rang. It was my daughter. "Papa is not going to make it through the night." The phone was put to my father's ear and I spoke to him these final words. "Hi Dad, it's Kathy, I love you with all my heart, I'll be home soon." I wanted to cry out "wait for me," but didn't.

Somberly, packing began as I angrily recalled being told he would live another six months. If only I had known I wouldn't have left him. The night air was cool as I carried the last suitcase across the dimly lit parking lot to where my husband stood loading the car when my cell phone rang. It was my sister. "Dad's gone," she said calmly, ever so gently and with all the composure she could muster. "He went peacefully, we were all here with him."

I dropped the suitcase on the black-tarred lot and walked toward the far end of the condo complex as if running away, sobbing, not able to catch my breath, still clutching the phone tightly to my ear unable to speak. I never felt so alone.

Unable to sleep that night I arose slowly then quietly left the bedroom so I wouldn't wake my husband. He would have a long drive home tomorrow. I sat up alone for hours that night on the balcony snuggled into a chair holding my robe tightly around me. Looking out at a cloudless night with the stars twinkling brightly and the moon ghostly illuminating the ocean, its sandy beach and all the high-rise condominiums, I tried desperately to feel my father's freed spirit praying that he would come to me and say goodbye. He never came.

Elsie had loved Bob since she was a mere child of 15 and wondered how after 65 years of marriage she could ever survive such intense sorrow. Elsie was very devoted to her husband and every day for over three years she would visit him. She spoke of that last visit.

"When I walked into the room, he sat up in bed, his eyes lit up and sparkled as they always did when he smiled. He kissed me and said, 'I've been waiting for you'. I sat in a chair beside his bed; he took my hand, held it tightly, never letting go. He went to sleep and never woke up. Why didn't I know that he was slipping away? I didn't realize until later that he must have been waiting for me to come in before leaving. His kiss was his way of saying goodbye."

The love and support of her four daughters was comforting, yet they recognized that with their mother's profound loss came the desire to reunite with her brothers, of returning home to her birth place, to reminisce of happy times gone by.

That September of 2008, my husband and I surprised my mother with a month long trip to Florida for a family reunion. She hadn't seen her brother Russell for eight years, and neither she nor Russell had seen their half brother Clyde in 20, not since their eldest half brother Phil had passed away in 1988.

Today was going to be a happier occasion and I was filled with anticipation. One by one the families began to arrive at about 10:00 a.m., gathering together on the eighth floor of the Canaveral Towers Condominiums overlooking the expansive blue Atlantic Ocean glittering brightly in the sun.

Mornings brought beautiful golden sunrises, never replicated, and the fishermen were always the first to arrive at the beach to firmly plant their poles in the sand, hopeful of making a boastful catch. The ever-present seagulls were seen preying, swooping haphazardly about in order to take advantage of any promising prospect. The early risers were out taking their brisk morning walk along the water's edge and further out the surfers were sitting on their boards patiently waiting for the swelling ocean to form the perfect crest upon which to ride. The white sandy beach would soon be speckled with colorful umbrellas and squealing children, as they would clumsily leap over the salty breaking waves.

Standing on the balcony you could feel the warmth of the sun shinning on your face. It would be necessary to squint your eyes to gaze at the pelicans flying in formation directly overhead; curiously seeming to always fly north. The eighth floor is also a great vantage point to watch the shuttle lift off from the Kennedy Space Center. The spectacular nighttime launches never fail to attract crowds that jam-pack the beach and surrounding area to capacity.

From their homeport in Cape Canaveral, you can watch the cruise ships sail away. The Disney ship, for one, can be seen as it pulls away playing "It's A Small World After All" to the excited passengers on board heading toward the Caribbean. The ship becomes smaller and smaller until finally it disappears into the horizon.

There was excitement in the air as everyone greeted one another with warm embraces. Some family members were meeting for the very first time. They were all curious about their relationship to the Houstons and the Stewarts and eager to learn about the historical events their ancestors participated in and about the people that crossed their paths. Yet there were underlying questions that remained on the faces of the three siblings. There were questions each had about the others; but all had a deep seeded longing to understand their father and how he affected their lives and their relationship with each other.

To help them understand, I slowly began to systematically reveal their wonderful heritage. From Baden, Germany to Potosi, Wisconsin; Wurtsboro, New York; Chicago, Illinois; St. Louis, Missouri and then on to Eau Gallie, Florida where I uncover the compelling and unique events through time that made their father, William Phillip Roesch, the man he became, the choices he made and why, knowing it would change their lives forever; it did mine.

Sibling Reunion

Lunch consisted of homemade potato salad and BBQ chicken, cold cuts of ham, roast beef and turkey, and rolls. There were also potato chips, pickles and olives. Fresh fruit of strawberries and cantaloupe, and apple pastry sat on the table for dessert with a variety of cold drinks from which to choose. A lovely bouquet of flowers sat in the middle of the linen covered round table.

Conversations began slowly; photos and family trees were gazed upon and discussed. Laughter was now predominant as they realized they were so much alike. The Roesch dry sense of humor certainly was one trait that had been passed down through the generations, along with soft-spoken voices, suspenders for men and a beard no less. Pictures were taken to record the event, especially of the three remaining Roesch siblings. It happened rather quickly, the feeling of being familiar and comfortable.

Sibling Reunion
Russell, Elsie and Clyde, September 13, 2008

It was a wonderful, sunny warm and breezy day that 13ᵗʰ day of September 2008. Before the visit came to an end they embarked upon a journey together, back to their grandfather's house, the Roesch House in Eau Gallie. More family pictures were taken inside the home; then they strolled the grounds, seeing the winter homes of their great grandfather Philip and of their great uncle, Clyde. A leisurely stroll was taken by all through the family Houston Cemetery, mourning that so many stones were now gone.

The house on Old Oak Street where Elsie lived as a child, no longer exists. She remembered living and playing with her cousin, Ora Lee Seawright, now Palmer, in this close-knit neighborhood. They are both great-granddaughters of John Carroll Houston III. Others were seeing it all for the very first time. Ora Lee recalled how "they always called her Elsie Louise and they always called me Ora Lee."

The time had come once again, just as it had in history past, there were embraces to say goodbye. Yet, something had changed. A connection of love had been made and they reached an understanding of their father and all that had gone on before; this was their new beginning.

Epilogue

The search for the Roesch family had one more story to tell. The call of find me could not be silenced. There would be no resting until their burial sites were found.

I wondered if it were possible these missing family members were interred in the Houston Family Cemetery and their markers destroyed and lost forever when it was vandalized. Then it was discovered that after the year 1910 the town would no longer permit burials in the Houston cemetery. From this date forward it was decreed that the new Eau Gallie Cemetery established in 1902 was to be used.

There I found many gravestones of Houston and cousins named Stewart, all with a special history of their own. I found only one Roesch relative identified with a stone, it read, William P. Roesch, May 1893-1960, my grandfather, with the Masonic Lodge emblem engraved upon it. There seemed to be space on this plot for the others. One could make a logical assumption that other family members were here too, but without a maker how could I know for sure.

It is important to note here that it was in 1969 that Melbourne and Eau Gallie citizens voted for unification of their towns. So there is no longer an Eau Gallie; it is all Melbourne, The Harbour City. But, you still find citizens that take pride in their community of Eau Gallie and will call it that until the day they die. Everywhere you look, the name is still seen on signs, buildings and churches. The town is loved by all who know her or live there.

My search began in the Cocoa and Titusville, Florida libraries, going through reels of old newspapers on microfilm. Long arduous hours were spent when finally, one by one, obituaries were found. The articles gave clues as to where they died, family members, pallbearers if any, in what church the services were held and perhaps the city or town where they were laid to rest.

One helpful clue was uncovering the name of the funeral parlor that serviced the family, the Brownlie-Maxwell Funeral Home in Melbourne, Florida, still in business since 1915.

A visit was made to the funeral home to request a search for five names. Michael and Ryan Brownlie were both so very helpful. A week later the call came, yes, their records proved that William Russell Roesch and his step-daughter Eva Lena were indeed in the Eau Gallie Cemetery. Unforunately, the years that would have included the other three were missing.

Death certificates were obtained in the hopes of finding additional information. If William Russell is buried there, then his wife Ada surely must be. And, where records show that his step-daughter Eva Lena was beside him, then her husband, Clarence E. Dean is there. The last would be Nellie, who tragically died so young, the first wife of William Phillip, the mother of young Phil. She was the first loved Roesch in Eau Gallie to die; of course, Nellie surely must be there, too. And there it was, on the death certificates of Ada and Nellie: place of burial, Eau Gallie.

Here I am at the end of a facinating jouney, not only discovering a remarkable history, but receiving the wonderful gift of knowing my ancestors. It changed me in ways that I never expected; it gave me a sense of honor of being part of something unique.

The realization that because they had no marker erroneously gave the impression they never existed and somehow they didn't matter. They did indeed exist and they lived their lives the very best they could, sometimes under very difficult and painful situations. They contributed during their lifetimes by shaping their communities and forming the future based on the ideals they taught their children. I have been blessed with a special opportunity to validate and memorialize their honorable lives.

A granite stone was placed in front of the gravestone of William Phillip Roesch, a gift from Elsie Louise Roesch Smith, Clyde Wilson Roesch and Kathryn Marie Smith Lockhard.

WILLIAM R. ROESCH
1866 – 1941
ADA HOUSTON ROESCH
1857 – 1924
CLARENCE E. DEAN
1861 – 1928
E. LENA ROESCH DEAN
1876 – 1942
NELLIE OSBORNE ROESCH
1892 – 1924

You are no longer lost. Rest In Peace.

Reflections

Quiet moments by the riverside reflect
to me my being. Awoke did I this spring
aware of this existance within me.
Could I have been on that branch
wrapped in silk as if a cocoon?

Why have I slept so many a spring when
I find life so alive within me.
This day the sun was too warm,
too bright and rose up ever so gently
that I found myself aroused,
so stired that I burst into being.

All around the riverside nature
·is alive and we are one.
My blood rushes as the river,
my heart beats to the song of the birds,
my hair blows as the limbs of the trees do sway
and my touch is gentle as a petal on a rose.

Nature cares for itself and it will care for me,
and I have no fear for what's to be.
Quiet moments by the riverside reflect
to me my being. Awoke did I this spring,
aware of this existance within me.

Kathryn Smith Lockhard

DOCUMENTS

Franz Rösch German Passport–December1854

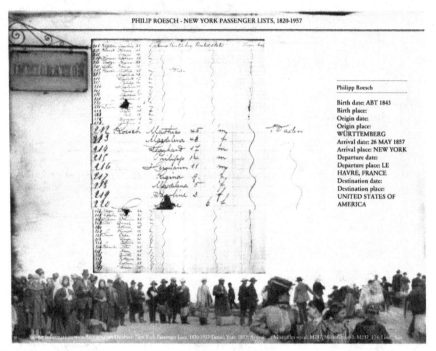

The Wm. Nelson
NY Passenger list of The Roesch Family

POST OFFICE DEPARTMENT,
CONTRACT OFFICE,

WASHINGTON, *June 20*, 187*1*.

SIR:

To enable the Topographer of this Department to determine, with as much accuracy as possible, the relative positions of Post Offices, so that they may be correctly delineated on its maps, the Postmaster General requests you to fill up the spaces and answer the questions below, and return the same, verified by your signature and dated, under cover to this Office.

Respectfully, &c.,

Giles A. Smith

Second Assistant Postmaster General.

TO POSTMASTER AT *Eau Gallie*
Brevard Co.
Florida

The (P. O. Dept.) name of my office is *Eau Gallie*
Its *local* name is *Arlington*
It is situated in the *North East* quarter of Section No. *21*, in Township *27* (north, south), Range *Thirty Seven* (east, west), County of *Brevard*, State of *Florida*.
The name of the most prominent *river* near it is *Indian River*
The name of the nearest *creek* is *Elbow Creek*
This office is *on* said river, on the *West* side of it, and is *on* said nearest creek, on the *North* side of it.
The name of the nearest office on route No. is *Sand Point* and its distance is *22* miles, by the traveled route, in a *Northerly* direction from this my office.
The name of the nearest office, *on the same route*, on the other side, is *St Lucie* and its distance is *53* miles in a *Southerly* direction from this my office.
The name of the nearest office *off the route* is , and its distance by the most direct road is miles in a direction from this my office.
This office is at a distance of from the Station of the Railroad, on the side of the railroad.

State, under this, the names of all other offices near your office, in different directions from it, and their distances from it by the most direct roads.

* If the town, village, or site of the Post Office, be known by another name than that of the Post Office, state that other name here, that it may be identified on the map of the State (or Territory).

☞ A *diagram* of the township and sections (or, where the land is not so divided, a sketch map), showing the precise location of your office, together with the adjoining Post Offices, towns, or villages, the roads, railroads, and larger streams or creeks, in addition to the above, will be useful, and is desired.—*See diagram blank accompanying this, to be filled up.*)

(Signature of Postmaster.) *John C Houston P.M.*

(Date.) *July 9th 1871*

John Carroll Houston, Postmaster

William & Ada Marriage Certificate

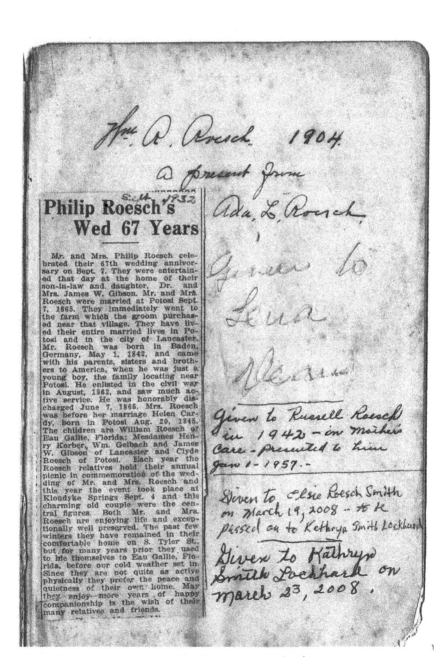

Wm. R. Roesch   1904.

a present from

Ada. L. Roesch,

Given to

Lena

Roesch

Given to Russell Roesch
in 1942 – in Mother's
Care – presented to him
Jan 1– 1957.–

Given to Elsie Roesch Smith
on March 19, 2008 – to be
passed on to Kathryn Smith Lockhard

Given to Kathryn
Smith Lockhard on
March 23, 2008.

Bible Ada gave as gift to her husband,
William Russell Roesch

145

The United States of America,

481

TO ALL TO WHOM THESE PRESENTS SHALL COME, GREETING:

Homestead Certificate No. 11955

Application 22859

Whereas there has been deposited in the GENERAL LAND OFFICE of the United States a CERTIFICATE of the Register of the Land Office at Gainesville, Florida, whereby it appears that, pursuant to the Act of Congress approved 20th May, 1862, "To secure Homesteads to actual settlers on the public domain," and the acts supplemental thereto, the claim of William R. Roesch has been established and duly consummated in conformity to law for the North West quarter of the South West quarter and the South half of the South West quarter of Section eighteen and the North West quarter of the North West quarter of Section nineteen in Township twenty-seven South of Range thirty-seven, East of Tallahassee Meridian in Florida, containing one hundred and sixty acres.

according to the Official Plat of the Survey of the said Land returned to the GENERAL LAND OFFICE by the SURVEYOR GENERAL.

Now know ye, *That there is therefore granted by the UNITED STATES unto the said William R. Roesch the tract of Land above described: TO HAVE AND TO HOLD the said tract of Land, with the appurtenances thereof, unto the said William R. Roesch and to his heirs and assigns forever.*

In testimony whereof I, Grover Cleveland President of the United States of America, have caused these letters to be made Patent, and the Seal of the General Land Office to be hereunto affixed.

Given under my hand, at the City of Washington, the fifth day of February, in the year of Our Lord one thousand eight hundred and ninety-six, and of the Independence of the United States the one hundred and twentieth.

[L.S.]

By the President: Grover Cleveland

By M. McKean *Sec'y.*

L. Q. C. Lamar, Recorder of the General Land Office.

General Land Office of the United States of America
Officially transfers 160 acres from John Carroll Houston
To William Russell Roesch, dated February 5, 1896

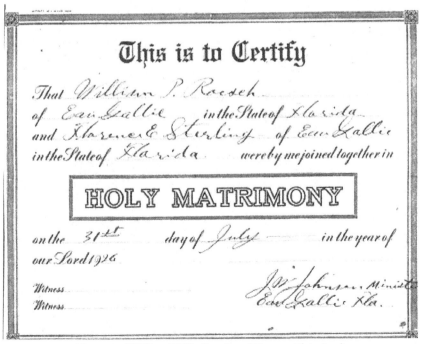

Eau Gallie Record January 17, 1924

Marriage of William Phillip Roesch and Florence Eloise Sterling

Postcard of Rocky Water Park

Emond Lewis Sterling's Business Card

Eau Gallie Woman's Club 1935-1936

GRAND CHAPTER OF FLORIDA
ORDER OF THE EASTERN STAR

Melbourne Fla _5/25_ 19_42_

This is to certify that

Sr. Lena Dean

whose name is signed in the margin, is a member in

good standing of _Melbourne_ Chapter No. _106_

and has paid dues through _Dec. 31_ 19_42_

Maria Sidwell Secretary.

No. _35_   Amount _2.00_

Eva Lena Roesch Dean
Eastern Star Membership Card 1942

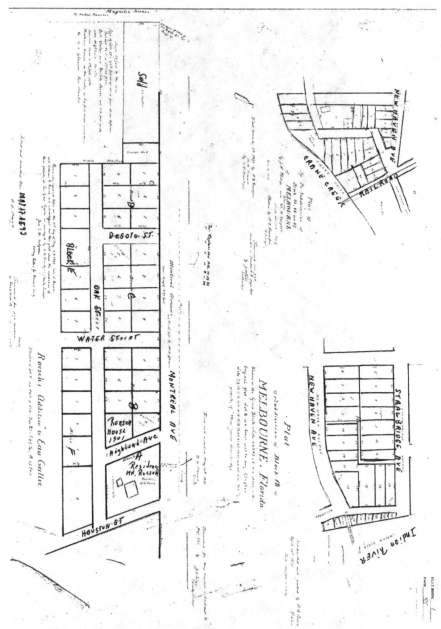

Roesch's Addition to Eau Gallie, map listing property of William R. Roesch, dated, May 17, 1892, Residence, Mr. Roesch, Block A is the location of J. C. Houston's slave quarters and first residence of William and his wife Ada. Today Block A is site of s the Rossetter House. Across the street in Block B, is the home William built in 1901, the Roesch House.

An early 1900 booklet that belonged to Florence Sterling Roesch Hilligoss. She signed her name along the top. Published by the Photo Place. It tells the story of Eau Gallie's accomplishments, history, fishing, transportation, boating & water sports, school & church's, graves, gardens and farms, It's location, health, conditions and surroundings, and it's future. The remainder of the book are old photographs of all the historic buildings in Eau Gallie, including Roesch's Highland cottages on Highland Avenue.

WAR VETERAN BECOMES CITIZEN AT AGE OF 95

—Courtesy of Telegraph-Herald.

Philip Roesch, 95-year-old Lancaster, Wis., Civil War veteran, is shown above at the right as he was being congratulated by Circuit Judge Sherman E. Smalley of Cuba City, Wis., on the occasion Monday of Mr. Roesch becoming a naturalized American citizen. Judge Smalley's father was captain of the Civil War company in which Mr. Roesch served.

Philip Roesch, Civil War Veteran
Becomes Citizen at Age 95

About the Author

KATHRYN SMITH LOCKHARD is a former financial controller. She has spoken to large academic groups on career education and assisted in writing a manual for the State Department of Education based on statewide surveys she had conducted. As a videographer hobbyist, she has been interviewed on radio. As a direct descendant of the Roesch and Houston families, she has given a presentation to members of the Brevard Historical Society on the Roesch history based on three years of arduous research and countless interviews. A native of Florida, born at the former Banana River Naval Air Station, she now makes her home in Massachusetts with her family.